Starting and Operating a Home-Based Business

Starting and Operating a Home-Based Business

HD
62.5
. E95
1990
West

David R. Eyler

WILEY

John Wiley & Sons

New York • Chichester • Brisbane • Toronto • Singapore

Library of Congress Cataloging in Publication Data:

Eyler, David R.
    Starting and operating a home-based business / David R. Eyler.
       p.   cm.
    Includes bibliographical references.
    ISBN 0-471-51037-8. — ISBN 0-471-51036-X (pbk.)
    1. New business enterprises. 2. Home-based businesses.
  I. Title.
  HD62.5.E95 1989
  658.1′141—dc20   89-36240
                                         CIP

Printed in the United States of America

90 91 10 9 8 7 6 5 4 3 2 1

To my parents,
Eunice and Charles Eyler,
for the gifts of a loving home
and an enduring work ethic.

Preface

We have come full circle. The reasons for working in collective settings on scheduled shifts are becoming less compelling with each passing day. Before the industrial age, people worked at home because there was no outside system that required more than occasional participation in group situations. We are working at home again today because the vast networks of modern commerce and technology are available at home—electronically.

Even if you are not a computer buff, don't exclude yourself from consideration as a home-based worker. The information revolution is a surprisingly broad concept. Being able to profit from the computer-related technology depends primarily on your ability to let it serve you in whatever it is you do well. This book contains chapters describing how the new, user-friendly technology has made it possible to sell, provide professional services, and even manufacture in home-based settings. You will see how your own specialty—or one that you are very much interested in learning—might reasonably be fashioned into a one-person business start up in your own home.

Professionals of every type can now acquire and master relatively inexpensive consumer-oriented computer technology that will let them produce impressive results at home. Everything from precision milling for the space shuttle, to composing music, producing videos, researching arcane subjects—or efficiently processing the words of others for profit can be done at home. You might be surprised at how many seemingly sophisticated services and production processes—of corporate giants and small firms alike—are actually done from someone's electronic cottage, some of it while still on the payroll, some by independent contractors or corporate entities whose only smokestack rises from the fireplace in their den.

If your talents can be related in any profitable way to the information revolution—and I will show you how they almost certainly can—you can arrange to do all or part of your work from home. It is not necessary to make an immediate choice between your present job and becoming a full-time, home-based worker. The change can take place over time as you make a reasoned transition from full-time employee with a growing part-time start up, to being the master of a burgeoning business that clearly justifies ending your commute to the office permanently.

If you are further along and have already made the commitment to a full-time endeavor of your own, this book discusses the economies and conveniences of the home office approach as a prudent way to begin and grow. Go back to your business plan and start penciling out the monthly office rent and utilities, the receptionist, and all of the furnishings and equipment that you feel you must have in a "proper" office. Add to that the cost of commuting—both monetary and the hour or two of aggravation and lost productivity each day—and lunch, and parking, and more—and you have some very apparent reasons for the growing popularity of working at home. These factors can mean the difference between surviving long enough to reach profitability before running out of capital, or going under prematurely by unnecessarily enriching a lot of supporting facilities and services that you really did not need.

Approached correctly, the home-based business can provide a unique combination of advantages and economies that cannot be found in any other kind of small business start up. There is a body of knowledge and tricks of the trade that have become sufficiently defined and important to warrant your attention. Newsletters are published and suppliers now cater to the professionals who offer their services in this mode. This new pool of information and considerations can have a real impact on your success or failure.

For every one piece of useful guidance, it seems, there are two experts trying to capitalize on your thirst for knowledge and assistance in starting a business. This book will provide you with both the good news and the bad news in matters relating to everything from the choice of legal organization—which, contrary to the popular wisdom, may be anything but obvious—to marketing your services or shopping prudently for technology.

The lifestyle of the home-based worker is not for everyone and you would be well-advised to conduct a thorough self-appraisal before leaping. On the other hand, there are ways to successfully cope with nearly all of the shortcomings of working from home. Whether your problem is where to find the space to do it, or how to stay in the loop with your professional peers and customers, I offer advice born of years of experience that will help you.

Accept my invitation for a guided tour of the newly sophisticated world of the home-based worker of the very late twentieth century. Let me show you how everyone from the Internal Revenue Service to the local zoning board will help you to achieve your goals (or at least not interfere with them)—if you know how to ask the right questions and give the informed answers that sort you out from the unscrupulous, and often naive, operators they seek to control. Let a thorough knowledge of the burgeoning working-at-home industry guide you to a successful place in it, full or part time, as you choose.

DAVID R. EYLER

Washington, D.C.
November, 1989

Contents

Introduction

Homework isn't just for students anymore! When it takes the form of an adult earning a substantial income at home, it is by no means limited to independent specialists who often spurned the office complex for the convenience of their own residences and studios. The bookkeepers and clerical people are still there, as are the artists and stock market gurus—but they have a lot of company now. Twenty-seven million other people do the same thing, if you count both full-time and part-time (Tooley, 1989).

A GROWING TREND

The modern trend toward home-based businesses reflects a wide diversity of occupational callings. The dream of working at home is more nearly within the grasp of today's office dwellers. This is because more and more of them are dealing in information, a highly portable, transmittable commodity that is the essence of the computer and telecommunications revolutions that continue to bring landmark changes, first to our workplaces and now our homes. The necessity for these two—workplace and home—to be physically different places is fading.

If you have considered the desirability of leaving the daily commute behind and working at home, you are anything but the exception. According to a recent Roper poll, of the people who responded that at least some of their work could be done at home, two-thirds

1

said they would like to have that flexibility. Among those whose occupations were not compatible with home-based work, fully one-third were interested in learning a new job that would let them take advantage of the idea ("Computers and the Work Place: Interest in Working at Home Still Strong," 1988).

MANY WAYS TO WORK FROM HOME

As later chapters reveal, there are infinite ways to approach home-based work. A great deal of attention has been focused on two aspects of the phenomenon that no longer constitute either its core or most dynamic growth segment. These are telecommuting as an employee of someone else's company (a concept developed more fully in Chapter 4), and at-home clerical and apparel workers that are the periodic focus of high profile labor movement attempts to "end their exploitation."

Telecommuting continues to grow as hundreds of companies experiment with its possibilities for achieving economies for the firm and desired conveniences for the employees, but telecommuting is not on the verge of replacing the traditional workplace anytime soon. In the realm of home-based production piecework, one person's "exploited worker" is another's willing contributor to the economy free of reporting to the mill or steno pool. The issues are complex and variable.

The skyrocketing phase of the work-at-home movement is the entrepreneur. These self-starters use it as an economical, private, and efficient way to test and incubate the thousands of new businesses that breath new life into the economy every business day. Many choose to start as executive moonlighters, quietly starting their businesses and verifying their profitability in the comfort and privacy of their residences. Others simply sever their ties with full-time positions in the traditional workplace and launch ventures of their own with a total commitment of time and resources.

Being technology and communications literate, a new generation of home-based workers has discovered that their residential neighborhoods can be the perfect place to start clean, nondisruptive businesses. As these enterprises grow, the home businessperson faces decisions on how to accommodate growth within the home. In-house technology and service-oriented solutions that can stave off returning to traditional commercial settings are discussed in the chapters to come.

THINGS YOU NEED TO KNOW

Tax advantages rank high among the reasons for making your home your place of business as well. Home is already the biggest investment and tax-saving device for the average person, and a properly conceived and operated home-based business makes it even more so.

The IRS constantly struggles to balance its twin congressional mandates to end abuses and, at the same time, encourage the development of legitimate small business ventures. It is a complex issue that requires constant attention in order to receive your share of the breaks and remain on the right side of the law. The business organization and tax chapters give you the insights to appreciate the sea in which these regulators swim. The rules may change, but you will be able to understand what is going on, how it impacts your home business, and how to adapt successfully.

If your attempt at home-based work takes you beyond being someone else's employee, you will need to understand the ramifications of representing yourself as an independent contractor. Whether trying to protect yourself from an exploitative employer who is attempting to avoid paying you benefits or, more likely, if you want to take advantage of the wonderful freedom it provides for the in-demand professional, you need to know the rules. Chapter 10 familiarizes you with what the IRS looks for in an independent contractor.

Naive home-based start ups can waste time, energy, and money by not following the required regulatory procedures. There are ways around almost any problem, but you must know the sensitivities and cast your solutions in a light that will ensure approval. Chapter 12 gives you the basis for writing your own checklist of local concerns and advises you on the proper approach to keeping the neighbors and public servants on your side—or at least avoid their active opposition to your plans.

Insurance is one of the areas that becomes complex when you start doing business from your residence. Again, the solutions are seldom difficult or prohibitively costly, but you need to know what questions to ask, which risks to insure, and what exposures to take your chances with, or "self-insure." Chapter 14 reviews the basics of small business risk management. Using this information, you will avoid such potentially disastrous mistakes as voiding your home or vehicle insurance by using either property for business purposes without the approval of your insurer.

Creating a working space in your home is both an exercise to be savored, and a quagmire of potentially costly mistakes to avoid. By following the guidance provided in Chapter 5, you can get down to the basics of what you really want, need, and can afford. Examine your options thoroughly at the outset and appraise their potential. The illustrations shown in this book range from richly appointed home offices delivered by freight from prestigious national mail order firms, to economical office furnishings that are designed to be strapped to the top of your car and assembled at home.

NEW POSSIBILITIES FOR HOME-BASED WORK

Once you have mastered the concept of the independent contractor and know the basics of business organizations and their tax treatment, you are ready to market your services. You owe yourself an open-minded look at the fantastic possibilities that have opened up in recent years, both in your field and in others that you may find attractive.

Selling from the home in the new age can be much more than insurance or real estate sales. There is nothing wrong with those possibilities when you give them a modern twist, but don't skip Chapter 7 because you thought you could never be a salesman. Sophisticated marketing possibilities abound that amount to a very systematic and efficient application of marketing demographics and technology-enhanced selling, order taking, and fulfillment. It is worthwhile reading just to become familiar with what can be done to market your own nonsales related services.

Production from the home is also totally new in terms of its sophistication. With the computerization of so many processes, not much in the way of specialty manufacturing is beyond the reach of the properly situated home-based business. Chapter 9 introduces you to the new ways of thinking, rather than attempts to provide blueprints for a few home-based production businesses. Given this nudge in the right direction, if you are so inclined and have an area of expertise, you will have little trouble pursuing the details within your own specialty's associations and suppliers.

Professional services lend themselves particularly well to home-based delivery with the assistance of consumer-priced communications and computer technology. Technology cuts both ways in that it: (1) makes it possible to roam the country electronically and perform your service with a professional, computer-supported image, and (2) continually spawns a variety of subspecialties in which you can offer new services (e.g., by becoming a consultant and showing small companies how to implement voice mail, or fax, or whatever is about to hit the market next.) The word *professional* is used in its broadest sense in Chapter 8 by telling you how to open your thinking to a full range of service possibilities that would work well from a residential base.

You are considering home-based work at an exciting time, rich with possibilities for both the

- Independent employee who wants to stay on the company payroll, buy enjoys the flexibility of working at least part time from home; and the
- Entrepreneur looking for a way to get started without the potentially devastating overhead of commercial space and all that goes with it.

Regardless of where you find yourself among the possible applications of these emerging work and business lifestyles, it is a time of great opportunity for people with the knowledge to do it right. *Starting and Operating A Home-Based Business* will tell you what you need to know and give you the advantage of a fast, efficient start on your personal road to success.

Chapter 1

There Has Never
Been a Better Time

The time is right to follow your personal and professional instincts regarding where and how you want to make a living. There now exists a previously unrealized combination of factors that will permit you to:

- Select the part of the country from which you wish to offer your services
- Make that decision totally independent of the existence of a job opening in someone else's company
- Transition your way to successful self-employment without the costs, complications, and risks of a traditional business start up
- Use modern business and communications technology that will make your business easily transportable to your ultimate geographic location
- Live a combination work and leisure lifestyle of your own design.

We live in an extraordinary time in which a person with in-demand skills and successful work experience can literally choose the venue of his or her labors.

JOIN THE GROWING TREND

Modern economies are driven increasingly by the services of skilled people. They are less dependent on the brawn of workers in the shrinking smokestack industries and trades. There is burgeoning opportunity for a variety of businesspeople who have experienced the contemporary workplace, understand how it functions, are literate in its terminology and technology, *and* perceptive enough to identify needs that can be met independently.

Trends are set by the practices of a society's more flexible members. Today, professionals and managers with the insight and independently valued skills to do so, are quietly stepping outside of organizations. Often they turn around and serve the needs of the very industries they left and they do it with more creativity, profitability, and satisfaction as home-based professionals.

"Some 27 million people now opt to commute to another room of the house either full or part-time, and a third of all new businesses registered in 1988 operate out of the home. The advent of the affordable personal computer, capable of turning out sophisticated graphics as well as processing words and numbers, has been the main impetus; by 1992, nearly a third of all households are expected to own a PC. But improved telephone technology, the growth of databases filled with every imaginable sort of information and the invention of personal facsimile machines and copiers also are making it easier to abandon the comfort of the corporate nest" (Tooley, 1989, p. 120).

As Figure 1–1 indicates, more than half of the home-based workers are there on a full-time basis and they are part of a steadily growing number. This group more than doubled during the 1980s and is projected to continue to increase at the same rate as we approach the twenty-first century.

The trend has not been lost on those who supply the equipment for home offices. Joanne Levine (1988) reports that the vendors of electronic equipment for the home-based worker market are creating a whole new industry of down-sized, less costly equipment. In 1987, the home office niche accounted for $1.9 billion in sales of facsimile machines, copiers, personal computers, word processors, typewriters, telephone systems, and calculators. A 37 percent increase was expected for 1988, paralleling the growth in all segments of the work-at-home phenomenon.

Figure 1-1 A growing trend of home-based businesses. (Copyright, Dec. 26, 1988–January 2, 1989, *U. S. News & World Report*)

WHERE IT CAN LEAD

Today your prospects for starting a successful, professional level business at home are significantly better than they have ever been. You can ease your way into a career change by defining a transitional path that suits your circumstances and goals. It can begin from the comfort of your own home office on a part-time basis—with your existing position and support systems intact. As your concept proves itself commercially, it can grow into a prosperous full-time home business. At that point, you face these pleasant choices:

- Stay put and enjoy what you have created, free from the burdens of a commercial office and support staff;
- Assuming that your clients can be served from anywhere with the support of the modern business technology discussed in this book, relocate to where you would *really* like to be—efficiently

moving your office and home together, and hardly missing a beat with your existing client base; or

- Go on to become a traditional business operation from the comfort of an established home-based enterprise—where you already live, or in another part of the country.

You don't have to limit yourself to the choice between a structured job in another person's company, struggling through a traditional business start-up, or opting for work far removed from the valuable skills nurtured during your organizational career.

YOUR SPECIAL ADVANTAGE

Managers, professionals, and skilled workers have prerogatives not enjoyed by the general workforce today. In the changing world of work, they are the Darwinian survivors, the ones with the adaptive skills needed to pursue a new course and prosper, rather than remain chained to the diminishing security of the traditional workplace.

It is more than their specific skills that separates them from the work-a-day crowd. They see potential where others see consumer gadgets. For example, they might be fascinated with the latest advances in telephone answering machines because they see business calls efficiently handled. The typical consumer is more apt to focus on personal convenience and is insensitive to the machine's profit potential. The personal computer with all its small business promise is more likely purchased to file recipes, support games, or provide an electronic shoebox for tax receipts, than to launch a serious home business. Impressive telephones with multiple lines, speakers, automatic dialers, and time and date stamped message recorders are all now mass marketed to the nonbusiness residential user.

This creates an opportunity for the serious home-based business person. There is a natural complement of interests existing. Thanks to the consumer market for the same applied technology, the home-based business can be powerfully outfitted to reach national markets with relatively inexpensive, high capability computer and telecommunications products.

The prerequisites for a successful home-based business call for certain conditions before an ideal opportunity occurs. These conditions include:

- A new medium of exchange. *Paper-based communications* of the past are yielding to the *electronic-based communications* of the future.
- A new user elite. The *verbal literacy* of the past assumes a lower economic value, unless the *technical literacy* needed to convey ideas in the new environment is also acquired.
- A new market and products. *Material consumables* of the past are being supplemented, if not replaced entirely, by *information consumables* of the future—we devour information as we once consumed "things."
- Prosperity and stability. These conditions allow the luxury of such progress.

All of these conditions exist as the twentieth and twenty-first centuries merge. You are uniquely positioned in the midst of the right circumstances for achieving a most satisfying application of your skills in the marketplace. Whether you do it with a totally independent application of your own special talents or choose to support traditional individuals and firms that will need help making the transition, there is a profitable niche for the home-based professional.

WHY IS IT POSSIBLE?

Paul Hawken (1987), a successful businessman, consultant, author, and host of a popular public television series on small business, points out that size is no longer an advantage in business.

> The movement today away from mass markets and mass production means that it is more difficult for a business to please everyone. One size does not fit all, if it ever did. . . . The entrepreneur can more easily produce products with a higher ratio of information . . . because she is more nimble. Small business can think faster, change more quickly, establish better internal communications, and tailor their products and services to smaller markets. . . . Big business has been lagging in the transition from the mass to the information economy because it cannot *buy* what is needed to make the transition. (pp. 46–47)

You have what big business lacks, *plus you know their game.* There is a place for you to profitably identify one or more of the endless residual markets resulting daily from the overly general mass marketing of the fat and happy giants. Don't overlook the giants themselves as potential consumers of your special way of doing things. They may need your services, but you might have to convince some of them.

HOW CAN YOU DO IT?

People like you have discovered that their skills can be applied independently and profitably without the support of a large organization —or its staff and facilities. Many have started as a home-based professional focusing energy and resources on establishing a solid demand for their services. It is a reasonable alternative to strenuously emulating a traditional business front. Here are three preliminary steps to start with:

- Possess (or acquire) the ability to offer a valued service that lends itself to efficient delivery with the support of modern business technology
- Define a market for those services and exploit it independently.
- Designate the home as the business location—whether buying, renting, relocating—to define a comfortable combination of personal lifestyle and economic reality.

When these steps have been taken, you have something to sell, the means to reach your market, and a place from which to do business.

The professional going into business with an unproven idea and constraints on time and resources needs a highly efficient operation. You have a home and there is a good chance that you already have the personal computer, telephone, and other real necessities of your trade. Forget about office rent, furniture leases, nonessential support staff, and all the unnecessary overhead of the traditional business start-up. Clients are more interested in your competence, reliability, and price (in that order) than in your office's location or ambiance.

If the company dress code is getting a little old fashioned, trade it for casual wear, except when you go calling on clients in *their* environment—if ever. More business is initiated, nurtured, and consummated by telephone, fax, and/or overnight delivery services everyday. The world can literally be your marketplace and your opportunity to prosper in it is limited only by your ability to define and cultivate a growing set of users for what you have to offer.

In the home-based mode of delivering professional services, you can choose whatever personal lifestyle suits your tastes. Using time zone sensitive marketing, you are free to be a morning person—or the opposite, if your prefer. The only remnants of business formality that need be a part of your day are the protocols and terminology used in the markets you have identified.

THE HOME-BASED PROFESSIONAL

Robert E. Kelley wrote a book called *The Gold Collar Worker* in 1985 describing a new class of employee that companies are having trouble satisfying. In his effort to identify the problem for firms wanting to retain such people, this management consultant described the new home-based professional and some of the things that motivate him to go on his own.

Many of the thoughts expressed in this section are derived from Kelley's analysis. If you see yourself in this image, you may be comfortable fashioning a home business for yourself. Whether full- or part-time, you will find it a refreshingly challenging outlet for your professional energies.

The kind of people Kelley had in mind were "knowledge workers," collectors, processors, and disseminators of information. These individuals have a tendency to base their security on their own professional competence, instead of on an organization. They are independent and will go into business on their own, if they aren't able to satisfy their goals within an organization—and today they are sufficiently in demand to do so.

One of the most significant differences that Kelley attributes to these workers pertains to the nature of their work—the freedom and flexibility with which they conduct it. Gold collar workers are complex problem solvers not satisfied with bureaucratic drudgery or mechanical routine. Imaginative and original—not docile and obedient—they operate in an environment of uncertainty where results are not always predictable and the feedback cycle can be long.

Kelley spoke to a broad spectrum of potential home-based professionals, but a number of qualities that he mentions also have applicability in the broader universe of home workers. You will see as this book develops, it is not necessary to *be* a computer specialist or a telecommunications specialist in order to base a successful home business on such supporting technology.

IT IS BEING DONE

The kinds of knowledge-based businesses that these professionals find themselves attracted to require less start-up funding than more conventional businesses. One of Kelley's examples is a home-based computer software company that can be established for less than a million dollars. There are ways to contribute independently to such an enterprise without an investment of that magnitude. Thousands of home-based businesses that benefit operationally from the products of such million-dollar start-ups only need a few thousand dollars to put it to work for them.

These investments contrast dramatically with what he estimates it would take to start an automobile plant—more in the $50 to $100 million range. Another advantage of technology-based start-ups is their ability to link together a team of professionals, each working from their home offices. Add to this the likelihood of well paid spouses to meet the basic living expenses and you have a class of workers privileged in several important respects when it comes to capitalizing on the home-base business opportunity. Kelley reminds us that Hewlett-Packard, Tektronix, and Apple Computer all started in garages with almost no capital. You can emulate the pattern on a lesser scale and still benefit handsomely from the concept.

"Spinouts" are another way that ambitious professionals start their own enterprises—in many cases, with the blessings and assistance of their employers. Control Data, General Electric, Campbell Soup, and Tektronix are cited as major firms who sponsor employees wanting to develop ideas independently. A sized-down application of the concept might be an innovative way for you to begin a home-based business that could complement your present job, possibly giving your employer an outlet for developing marketable products from expensive research that is incompatible with present corporate strategy—offer them a win/win proposition.

Kelley's *Gold Collar Worker* portrays a trend that parallels the potential career pattern of a home-based professional as he sums up the frustrations and the outlets of those he studied:

A number of gold collar workers are taking moonlighting one step further by quitting their jobs and becoming full-time free-lancers. Solo practitioners of every stripe—accountants, lawyers, and doctors as well as writers and artists—have long been accepted. The trend now encompasses artificial-intelligence researchers, computer programmers, librarians, and financial advisors. As one consultant said: "Something is wrong when I save a client over $1,000,000, my firm makes $200,000 off the project, and I only get paid $30,000 for my time spent on that project. My brain power is not being leveraged correctly for my personal return on my personal investment in it." Anyone whose skills are in demand can find enough employers to buy their time on a per-project, per diem, or retainer basis. The most cautious free-lancers attempt to diversity their streams of income and their client portfolios, including various types of work and governmental as well as private employers." (p. 86)

People are finding ways to respond successfully to the urge to exploit their talents independently. Working from home is a viable way to begin —and it may be the only place of business you will ever need.

A NEW PROFESSIONALISM

Home-based employment is now commanding a level of respect that was never associated with it in the past. The new professionalism is evidenced by the emergence of such things as national organizations dedicated to serving the *top* end of the home working market. One of these is the American Home Business Association (AHBA) of Darien, Connecticut (800-433-6361/203-655-4380). AHBA publishes a newsletter and provides services directed at the up-scale home office operator appreciative of the sophisticated application of technology, tax-advantaged business practices, and the benefits of adapting the latest business trends to their at-home enterprises.

Government is recognizing the home-based business as a significant growth area in the important small business segment of the economy that generates so many new jobs. Tax laws address the business use of the home. Huge agencies such as the Department of Defense grow sensitive to its potential for satisfying the special ambitions of military spouses whose transient lifestyles deny them traditional business opportunities (Schill, 1988).

The significance of home-based employment at this time emanates from the combined impact of its new sophistication, increased market penetration, and the breadth of its application across the national economy. Its practitioners are not the fringe exceptions that have always been associated with it—artists, writers, stock market wizards, and the like. Mainstream professionals and managers are now supplying important services to the most vital segments of the national business community. They are doing it with energy, inventiveness, efficiency, and profitability that energizes the economy a legitimatizes the place of *the new home-based professional.*

Chapter 2

Pluses and Minuses of Working at Home

The people filling the ranks of the new home-based professionals have choices. They could readily find positions in the traditional workplace. These home-based workers made a positive choice to work at home; they chose *not* to work in a traditional 9 to 5 job. Conversely, a price is paid for turning your home into your place of work. One person's plus may be another's minus, the discussion that follows gives you some basis for making a personal judgment of which situation might be the best for you.

THE "HAVING IT YOUR WAY" URGE

There are attractive freedoms associated with self-employment. They are all the more dramatic when exercised in the comfort of your own home. A home workplace has the potential for being one of the most thoroughly inspiring settings that you can imagine—or it can degenerate into unfocused activity that spells the death knell for a fledgling business. You have to sort this out and be honest with yourself regarding your ability to function effectively and prosper in the uniquely ambivalent atmosphere of the home-based business.

17

Even with the double-edged quality of the working-at-home op-portunity, a growing number of people are attracted to the idea. A 1988 Roper poll on the subject reported these findings:

> With the skyrocketing costs of commercial real estate and rapid advance-ments in computer technology—not to mention the scarcity of, and in-creasing need for, day care—the idea of moving workers into their homes where they can be plugged into the office via computer has appeal for employers and employees alike. Echoing sentiments expressed in 1985, large numbers of people continue to be interested in the work-at-home-concept.
>
> . . . All told, the concept has greatest appeal among the Baby Boom generation. A 53% majority of all 18 to 29 year-olds would either like to work full-time at home on a computer or learn a job permitting them to do so. A 46% plurality of 30 to 44 year olds concur. A majority of parents with young children also like the idea. ("Computers and the Work Place: Interest in Working at Home Still Strong," 1988, p. 4)

According to *U.S. News and World Report* (Tooley, 1989, p. 120), there is an ever-growing pool of potentially interested workers with

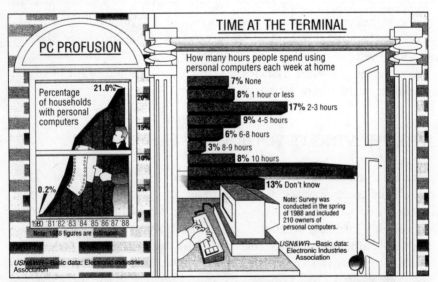

Figure 2–1 More home-based personal computer use. (Copyright, Dec. 26, 1988–January 2, 1989, *U. S. News & World Report*)

the skills and equipment to do the job—whether telecommuting, at-home staffers for someone else's firm, or self-employed entrepreneurs. Figure 2-1 graphically shows the growing proliferation of personal computer use in the home and the expectation that it will continue.

THE LITTLE THINGS—
DO THEY MATTER TO YOU?

We seek the liberties of self-employment and home office environment because of the shortcomings in the traditional workplace. Smoke curling up from the next partition wouldn't be an irritant or possible health threat at home. Hours of telephone gossip would consume neither resources nor your patience. These little things and a number of big ones, such as where you place your work priorities, seem more manageable in a home office that you personally control.

Use this sampling of traditional workplace "itches" to informally rate the value you place on the ability to control surrounding trivia. Don't get lost in the specifics as much as the general idea of escaping a class of life's irritations. For some, the ability to do so is a major plus—others would just as sincerely miss participating in these on-going social games—a minus that would call for some form of compensating activity at their home-based offices.

- *Denying biorhythms in the name of scheduled hours.* If you have always yearned to produce when the spirit calls, not when the alarm clock rings, the home office may free you of a barrier to your happiness and productivity—*assuming* the spirit still calls on a regular and profitable schedule.
- *Fresh air from a real window.* Modern office buildings rarely give you the luxury of throwing open the sash and breathing in whatever is there to inhale in your part of town. It's more important to maintain the climate-controlled efficiency that is boon to building engineers and bane to office workers from coast-to-coast. At home, it's your window to do with as you please.
- *Sharing common keyboards and mouthpieces.* Sounds trivial, but that is how most office sicknesses are spread. Ask any doctor. Your two most effective preventive practices are avoiding the source of infection and the frequent washing of your hands. At

home, the chances of doing both increase, but then there's the lessened opportunity to build desirable immunities.

- *Hygienic imperfections of group living.* Wouldn't it be nice to live in your own dirt and not someone else's? At home, it's all yours!

- *Length of breaks.* Working at home can mean the right to live without any schedules beyond those needed to interface with clients and get the job done. It's only your profit at stake, so the home-based professional is free to use that option to your own comfort and advantage—or ruin.

- *Music of your choosing.* The options at home include none, if that's what you prefer—welcome relief and a potential productivity booster for some who have long suffered the elevator music and worse!

- *Pools and parties—from football to farewells.* Always another round of peripheral events in which you should really participate. Will your life be better or worse without this semimandatory immersion in the lives of others? You just may miss such "belonging" activities—or maybe not? Don't despair, a surprising amount will still find its way to your door—at home— unless you are particularly insulated.

- *Someone else's good taste in your office furnishings.* Are you nonplused by the budget motel grade furniture you have endured for much of your professional life? How tolerant are you of the person who clandestinely does the office purchasing and appears with what he or she knows is best for you—the person with the power to run out of the "good stuff" just as your desk is reached. Despair no more—at the home office, you are the buyer, but then the bills come to you as well!

- *Staff meetings.* If they occur at all in your home-based business, it will be at your own discretion. You will have to gauge the impact of the lost interaction with others and arrange to replace it, if necessary.

- *The top button of your shirt.* Say goodbye to the mandatory necktie that conspired to restrict your higher level thinking. The home-based executive need not wear one.

- *To smoke or not to smoke—that is no longer a question.* The issue is moot and the choice your own—no small perk for either side in these days of strong feelings on the issue.

- *Two pairs of shoes per day.* Heels *and* sneakers will no longer be the norm, if your commute begins and ends at home. Personal preference and comfort, be it in footwear or anything else, will guide your selections. Real economies of comfort and costs may be realized working at home.
- *View—limited only your your means.* Carried to the extreme, a change of view can be accomplished by moving your desk to another window—or moving your window to another part of the world. The selection of home and office are one and the same for the home-based worker and limited only by your ability to afford the turf you long to survey.
- *Yielding to higher wisdom.* Snow closings become irrelevant to the home-office dweller. That's good and bad—no more bone-headed decisions by others to endure, but no more days off because the office is closed or inaccessible either!

These points are illustrative and not exhaustive. They serve only to trigger more relevant reasons why you would prefer to spend your working hours in your own environment—or what you would sorely miss. They range from large to small, or even petty, but they are the grains of sand that cumulatively change the course of careers, if the effected person has the power to choose. More of us do as the home office becomes an increasingly viable option, for an ever-widening group of people.

THE BIG QUESTIONS

Beyond the surface irritants lie the things more apt to effect your bottom-line happiness and productivity. After you have kicked the office cat and set the mood, to the extent that the physical realities of the dwelling and constraints of your budget allow, it's time to address things that matter less to you personally and more to you as a success-ful home businessperson. The plus or minus response on these issues is more telling in your appraisal of home-based business desirability.

- *Can you stay in the mainstream and remain current in your field?* Much of your professional currency comes from the day-to-day interaction with those in your specialty. There is the potential to lose some of that edge when you depart the traditional patterns of work, but it doesn't have to be that way. What will matter most is that you supply the initiatives needed to keep yourself in the loop professionally.

The plus side is that you can be more selective in your interactions, ignoring those that were of marginal value and opening up new avenues previously closed by employer-related restraints. The problem of isolation is real, but the solutions to it bring with them opportunities that outweigh the possible losses—if you recognize them and see to it that the necessary contacts are established and nurtured. The minus materializes if you are unable to sustain your industry knowledge from the outside looking in.

- *Can you remain in the path of new business contacts?* Service clubs and professional societies exist for the perpetuation of the interest groups represented. The furtherance of the business ends of the individual members is their reason for being, although some support worthwhile community activities as well. Depending on the nature of your home-based business, you will want to establish and maintain your involvement with those who buy your services.

  You are at no disadvantage in this regard because your office is in your home. Increasingly, the long distance nature of sophisticated home-based operations eliminates the need for local contacts entirely and leaves national professional meetings and day-to-day interaction in the marketplace as the most significant means of interaction. A minus only if your clients aren't amenable to this style of communication.

- *Will your specialty's technological state-of-the-art support a first-rate home-office operation?* The work-at-home revolution is fed by developments in technology. Whole home-based industries such as desktop publishing have been born of complementary computer hardware and software. When the relatively inexpensive home computer and high quality laser printer crossed paths with the software to let it lay out books and publications in a professional manner, an industry emerged that fit the home office nicely.

  Whether you face a plus or a minus rating in the area of technology readiness depends on your answers to questions such as these: Is your field supported by combinations of technological breakthroughs that lend themselves to home office exploitation? If it isn't, are you able to ply your trade successfully without specialty-specific technology (i.e., can you still do well enough supporting your efforts with the more general capabilities of modern information processing and communications?).

On the plus side, you either have the support readily available or have the opportunity to become the one to open the next technological door in your field by developing the applications software at home. A minus would register if the support were either not available, or general technology wouldn't give you sufficient support to market your skill competitively from home.

- *Are your skills in high demand, or can you generate business if it doesn't seek you out?* It isn't necessary to be a high technology master who is so much in demand that you are sought out by clients, but it would be nice! The reality for most is that you will function in competitive markets and your services will have to be dynamically sold to those not yet beating a path to your home office door. That isn't bad and should not limit your will to proceed. It does call for an honest self-appraisal regarding the essentials of self-promotion. Start-up enterprises, home-based or otherwise, usually find success critically dependent on their owner's ability to generate business.

  This is a big plus, if you are sufficiently in demand to ignore the marketing imperative, and a plus, if you are attracted to the task of self-promotion. It is a minus if you need it and are unable or unwilling to do it.

- *Will your clients accept you as a home-based operator?* The answer is a resounding yes, for most situations. The overwhelming concerns of most clients are usually competency, reliability, and cost effectiveness. The home-office is not a Madison Avenue suite and, if that image is required to do business in your field, a home office can't deliver. On the other hand, home offices can reflect a priceless blend of personal and professional good tastes rarely found in corporate settings—and a sense of privacy and dignity unrivaled by a commercial district.

  Many home-based professionals rarely see clients at their offices. Others gravitate toward a clientele that actually welcomes the individuality evidenced by the workstyle of the particular home businessperson's unique setting.

SOME LIKELY NET GAINS

Traditional workplace topics tend to follow you to your home-based business. Here are some things that you will probably find enhanced in your office operation.

- *Efficiency.* Increased personal efficiency and productivity should be among the bonuses received for the privilege of commuting to the next room. When a professional person takes to the home-based mode of operation, it is often with a zeal for the application of the latest in everything his field has to offer. At the traditional office, progress tends to be homogeneous—the one size fits all "let's go a little slower or faster than we individually are comfortable, so we can go together" mentality so common in group settings, isn't necessary at the home-based office.

- *Personnel.* Turn your copy of the personnel manual into a bookend and hire whomever you want, whenever they're justified, at whatever compensation level is mutually agreeable. It isn't quite that simple—if you have an employee of any kind, you will encounter obligations and limitations to your actions, but nothing like what you are used to in formal business organizations. This brings its own measure of efficiency. In the early stages—perhaps indefinitely—use outside services, temporaries, and independent contractors to eliminate your personnel problems.

    A possible minus from the personnel perspective is the loss of your comfortable place in a hierarchy. That is important to some people, and only you can judge what it means for your self-image and productivity. Another notable change is the lack of support staff. In your home-based business, you will be doing things for yourself that used to be handled by others. For some, it is a welcome relief to shorten the span of control—for others, attention to small tasks will be troubling and counterproductive.

- *Equipment.* A real plus in establishing a home office is the ability to maximize the use of the great stuff seen in trade publications and technology stores. Technology is the heart of the home-based office. Those who work there often choose to be surrounded by its most popular offerings. One drives the other: Technology makes the sophisticated home business operation possible; the home business provides a platform for the individualized exploitation of that technology's greatest potential.

Watershed breakthroughs for leading industries have occurred in home offices and garages. The great equalizer on today's business frontier is technology, and *most of it is right at home.* If you are not comfortable with new technology, you may have uncovered a large minus in your ability to thrive in the new home office environment.

New technology that can be operated from a home office assures a competitive starting position in almost any specialty. Such technology is within the reach of anyone knowledgeable enough to be aware of its existence and appreciative of its potential. With creatively applied technology, the home-based professional can project a powerful professional image to a national client base. That's a plus, if you are comfortable with the sources of this new power—a minus, if you're not.

- *Schedule.* Being able to work when your personal energy is at its peak is a tremendous advantage for the home-based professional. Discipline and long hours of diligent effort are not negated, but the power to produce when you are inspired to do so is no small benefit. The productivity of Thomas Edison and his peers was not built around office routine or rigidly defined times for receiving inspiration. You capture a measure of this creative initiative by pooling your living and working environments so that you can comfortably move back and forth between the two.

- *Commuting.* Remove this word, and its expense, from your repertoire. The greatest single home office efficiency in terms of time, money, and aggravation is the elimination of the dreaded trek to the office. With imaginative scheduling, your appointments can fit the nonrush hours and probably be combined into something less than a daily routine.

- *Travel.* Nothing says that business cannot be combined with pleasure. As a home-based business person with legitimate reason to call on clients in other parts of the country, you have personal choice and flexibility only dreamed of in most corporate travel planning. With only your personal bottom line to consider, it may make good financial sense to schedule the family vacation the week after your final client presentation in Florida.

Make the cost of your own personal round-trip business travel the benchmark and consider the possibility of some creative subsidy of overlapping personal travel.

- *Complementary Services.* Maintain reasonable separation between your business activities and your household services and expenses. That is not to say that there cannot be economies of scale. The service that does your domestic cleaning can do the same for your office and the costs pro rated fairly. The same approach can be extended to everything from the costs of operating your home to the care of the grounds that surround it, if a plausible case can be made for business necessity and even-handed distribution of costs achieved.

POSSIBLE DRAWBACKS

There are things about working at home that can be very inefficient. Many come in the form of distractions. Most lend themselves to corrective measures that include self-discipline, the proper physical layout, and the cooperation of others who share the residence. While the following list is not exhaustive, it highlights some of the areas that may require accommodation as you establish your home-based place of business.

- *Telephone.* At once your most vital link to the world and your downfall if you let it disrupt the flow of your business day. Such obvious solutions as answering machines and services conflict with the necessity to stay in touch, but they may prove to be essential. Another approach is to limit your "live answering" hours to certain times of day that you make known to those who seek you out. Periodic checks of the answering machine will allow you to return essential calls in a timely manner, saving the ones that can wait.

  Get a separate business line and limit its use strictly—no little people answering, unless your image is tolerant of such things.
- *Others in the home.* You love them dearly, but you are going to have to come to terms with how to avoid them during most of your prime-time business hours. The new found accessibility will be a blessing and a curse to you as a home-based professional who

will find it absolutely essential to draw an indelible line between home and home-office. Productivity and professional image demand nothing less.

The list could go on to include the mirror plus and minus sides of everything from home repairs to seasonal distractions—you save money, but it takes time/there's no place like home for the holidays, but will the business imperatives prevail? Suffice to say, we each have varying abilities to function well in the unstructured environments that are part of every home-based business day.

The point is that you must not overlook these realities. Try to undertake a hard-nosed appraisal of your capabilities as a self-manager. The candid opinions of a few individuals who know you well can provide worthwhile validation of your personal judgment. Unless a majority of these people see you quite differently than you see yourself, it's probably time to proceed with your plans!

Chapter 3

Adjusting to Working at Home

When you elect to work at home, you say a lot about what is important to you—in your life *and* work. The decision forces choices that will effect how successfully you pursue both your personal life and home-based business. It creates a hybrid environment that did not exist before in which the two most important components of your life meld more nearly into one. You concentrate the risks and potential rewards for both the personal and professional arenas—the focus for *most* of what matters to you happens at home. Special adjustments will be needed to maintain essential distinctions and avoid creating unnecessary tensions.

GETTING ALONG WITH A NEW BOSS

The face may be familiar, but the relationship won't be the same. The likeable guy you have sided with against a legion of imperfect supervisors is now your new boss. Every aspect of your performance, each brush with success or failure, will be under the scrutiny of life's least forgiving critic—you! As Figure 3-1 illustrates, the home office puts a lot of temptations well within your reach. Whether it is too much time on social calls or too much attention to your standing at the racquetball club, it will take discipline to keep your nose to the grindstone.

Figure 3-1 A comfortable, but temptation laden life style. (Photograph reprinted by permission of SOFTDISK PUBLISHING, publishers of DISKWORLD monthly software for the Macintosh)

Count on getting to know yourself very well as a solo act at the home office. Self-criticism can be more punishing than what you were used to getting from your harshest external critics. Like the rest of the working-at-home phenomenon, it has its good and bad sides—getting external feedback on a regular basis will demand perspective and some deliberate effort on your part.

Arriving at a satisfactory relationship with this new situation will include striking a reasonable balance on such things as:

- *Workload.* Over do it and you'll suffer from burnout; do too little, and you may not succeed.
- *Schedule.* A home-based eight to-five? Banker's hours? Or the complete freedom to work when the spirit moves you? It is up to you to make it satisfy the requirements of the bottom line.
- *Compensation.* Enough to make it worth your while, but with an eye toward surviving the slow times and providing for the reinvestment needed to grow.
- *Benefits.* Making the most of the organizational and tax angles to extract the indirect compensation that can make your home-based business rewarding.

- *Perks.* Funding the good life out of the company till calls for good judgment, and you are the one who must exercise it in your own business.
- *Travel.* Now that you are approving the vouchers, what is the relative worth of economy, business, and first class?
- *Vacation.* There definitely needs to be some, but how much and how do you leave the home office at home?
- *Performance evaluations.* Periodic face-to-face looks at how you are doing will be necessary and they have to go beyond checkbook considerations to include the things that didn't get a second glance in the traditional workplace—how is the job effecting your home life and are you accomplishing the personal goals you left the organization to achieve?
- *Your future with the company.* Is it working out and should you continue to pursue success, as you personally defined it, in the context of your home-based business?

If you can wrestle with such weighty issues and not upset the internal gyroscope that keeps you functioning, you and the new boss are going to make a great team. One priceless advantage of transitioning as a part-time home-based businessperson is learning the answers to some of these questions while your place in the traditional workplace remains secure.

Answering to yourself is a rare freedom. Client relationships and deadlines will still impose their external influences, but your interactions with the rest of the world will be largely on your own terms. Your successes will be the sweeter, desirable initiatives the less inhibited, and chosen relationships the more genuine, when they emanate from your own inspiration and direction.

CREATING A NEW OPERATING ENVIRONMENT

You won't be experiencing the morning ritual that for years has been preparing you for the task of getting down to business. The compulsive aspect of all of the symbolic behavior that took place by the numbers each workday morning will be diminished, gone, or, at the very least, optional:

- Alarm clock rings, the shower, the clothes
- Passage from your front door to the car pool, to the commuting route, to the parking garage, to the lobby, past security, to the elevator, past the receptionist, to your secretary, to your desk
- Office coffee, banter
- Work happens, phones ring, appointments are kept, and the day unfolds rather purposefully, with or without your initiatives.

A new set of motivators will have to set you off for a day of productive work at home. Bits and pieces of the familiar pattern may be retained, but expect an adjustment to a new way of getting (and keeping) the day rolling along.

Without detracting too much from the charm of the nonoffice home-based office that you have created, plan to set some expectations of yourself that will insure movement, such as establishing some time blocks or guidelines. For example, by:

- 9:00 A.M. you will have evolved from happy noncommuter enjoying a leisurely breakfast to a dynamic home-based professional insulated from all household distractions
- 9:30 A.M. at least one phone call will be placed to someone out in the world that will leave you feeling as though you are connected and proceeding as a part of the grand commercial scheme of things
- 10:00 A.M. you are into the project at hand, revising and creating and producing something of value that wasn't there when the day began
- 11:00 A.M. you are back on the phone confirming your mid-day appointments, again re-establishing your link with the mainstream and asserting your influence on what is going on out there, laying the groundwork for external processes that will reach back for your input in the not too distant future
- 12:00 Noon you are appropriately outfitted and on your way to a business lunch that will keep you face-to-face with the other half of your business equation
- 2:00 P.M. you are back at the home office checking a few things with associates in another time zone
- 3:00 P.M. receiving calls that make it necessary to get back to the West Coast associates at 5:00 P.M. their time/8:00 P.M. yours

- 4:00 P.M. off to an early evening with the family before returning to the planned 8:00 P.M. calls
- 9:00 P.M. exerting the restraint needed not to do more than note what must be done tomorrow, after wrapping up a stimulating hour on the phone regarding an exciting new project.

The flow of a productive day at the home-office is sometimes driven by external demands, but count on doing your part to keep the outside contacts fresh and alive. Home office phones don't necessarily keep ringing with outside offers, unless you stimulate the calls with a steady stream of initiatives that can find their way back to your doorstep.

As an independent professional, the cycle of a successful week is completed by seeing your worth affirmed by those with whom you sought to do business. Calls were returned and your input solicited. You were involved in other people's projects because your services were highly valued. That's the payoff that often matters almost as much as the dollars—no more treading water in someone else's preordained daily rituals.

It is good to know that the calls and handshakes were genuine, not based on the momentum of impersonal corporate relationships and obligations that tend to blur your identity and contributions. These rewards from your new operating environment are immediately dependent on your own competence and initiative—it is up to you to make them apparent in every home-based business transaction.

PROBLEMS AND SOLUTIONS

It would be unrealistic not to expect to make some adjustments as you switch over to the different psychological and social demands of the home-based office. Keep in mind that for every potential frustration there is a way to cope successfully. One way to go wrong in addressing the classic challenges of the home office workstyle is to expect the solutions to come from your traditional office experience. Here are examples of some typical problems and suggested cures:

- *Task avoidance.* A great curse of your new-found freedom as a home-based businessperson may be an inability to focus on the task that is going to put money in your pocket. There are so many other tempting things to do at home, and they have a way of presenting themselves as you are about to face something like a morning of difficult calls to new clients.

The interference isn't something that can be attributed to laziness. It generally takes the form of a worthy task that happens to be less objectionable than the one that should have priority at the moment. A home office is the perfect place to build the perfect database or write the ultimate mailing piece, when what is urgently needed is crunching the numbers for the analysis that will command dollars *now*.

Discipline is a component of the task avoidance solution, but it is not enough. The person with this problem is often a hard-driving, analytical professional who is being stymied by the kind of unstructured behavior that was easily buried in the traditional workplace. There the paycheck arrived with no clear link with immediate productivity. Analysis paralysis and working the nonprofit problem can be deadly in the less forgiving atmosphere of small business. Cash flow may have to take precedence over the expression of genius until that luxury can be afforded.

The answer lies in learning to set the hard nosed priorities associated with making a living as a home-based professional. Activity per se, even when brilliant, may have less than the desired result of the saleable productivity required to keep that home office open and you paying the bills.

• *Loneliness.* Those attracted to home-based work are usually more comfortable than most with their own company. A highly social person will have to anticipate compensating for what is essentially a quiet home-office atmosphere, but it can certainly be done.

Start with the choice of the appropriate business to operate from your home base in the first place. You can to set up an enterprise that has you out in the community most of the time, beginning and ending your day with an hour or two of office chores at home. In such situations, loneliness is hardly a problem. If the business doesn't lend itself to that degree of outside activity, consider the possibility of one that brings a desirably steady flow of visitors to your home-office door.

There are all sorts of gradations that can be achieved—the important realization is that you now hold the initiative for making or avoiding contact with the outside world. If you need more or less, be alert to the problem and turn the volume up or down accordingly. If it matters, don't ignore the problem when it surfaces. Remember, you are now on the outside looking in on traditionally initiated business social activity.

You have the special privilege of being selective in the ties you wish to sustain. How refreshing it can be to offer former colleagues an occasional neutral shoulder, free of the obligatory overtones that no longer need hinder these relationships. It is still a highly transactional world and there is plenty of opportunity to give and take. You just might have to be the one to keep the doors open since in your home office you may otherwise be out-of-sight, if not mind.

Some choose the quiet setting of the home-based office deliberately and revel in the fact that social contact is limited and purposeful—as defined by the individual operating the business. Isolation is a highly self-defined and relative term. Unless you sense a measure of social discomfort or find your business suffering from lack of contacts, the more private life of the home-based worker may simply be desirably different—not wrong or a source of concern.

• *Professional isolation.* Depending on your business, the necessary communication with your colleagues can be either intense or sporadic. In many fields, it is satisfactory to read—and perhaps contribute to— the professional literature. Add to that regular attendance at regional and national meetings and you have solved the problem. For others, immersion in the day-to-day dynamics of your field is required.

Your approach to maintaining the optimum level of association with your peers is individual, requires initiative beyond that formerly expected when someone else mandated your participation, but should be anything but impossible. Being a home-based professional places no limits on your ability to hold memberships and participate in appropriate activities. There are tax incentives for such activities and the travel associated with them that may be more meaningful as a private businessperson.

Yet another possibility for professional stimulation, beyond the more obvious feedback of regular interaction with associates by phone and in person, is electronic networking. As a home-based professional with a comfortable setting from which to exploit the potential of the computer used in other aspects of your business, now you can extend your professional networks via telecommunications. Electronic conferencing via your home computer equipped with a modem and a dedicated telephone line, is a way to stay active and even enhance your professional identity without ever leaving your home. Check with your professional associations and computer service companies like *CompuServe, GEnie, The Source,* and others for the existence of interactive networks that might link you to important sources of professional stimulation—and potential customers for your products and services.

- *"Homeaphobia."* Fear of being at home isn't a legitimate psychological problem, but the contrived term does describe a potential obstacle that can plague the home-based professional. There is a diminution of the ability to function in all phobic situations. Whether it is the closed space of the claustrophobic or the debilitating sensitivity to height of acrophobia, some people loose their effectiveness in certain settings.

Home-based workers assume a lot of responsibility for their own self-management. There won't be periodic conferences with supervisors regarding job effectiveness. It is now your problem to sense performance problems and deal with them.

Independent, highly productive individuals who tend to start home-based businesses carry with them the potential for their own discontent, even at home. They tend to be consumers of opportunity who devour it in great quantities and sometimes wonder where it has gone. At home, they will have to be the engine that continues to generate fresh challenges and opportunities.

The "homeaphobic" is the person who plunged into the home-office environment and used it up too quickly. Now you have things humming along smoothly and have time to notice the four walls around you and you aren't comfortable anymore. There is a shortness of breath or other manifestations of panic that say ". . . oops, I'm here in this house by myself and the world is going by without me! What do I do now? There is no hour-to-hour verification of my self-worth and I'm coming unglued!"

In the absence of sufficient self-satisfaction to keep it at bay, "homeaphobia" is cured by growth—business and personal. If you feel yourself experiencing the early signs, realize that you are at a plateau and plot your next move. It may involve a simple change of home-office routine or it could mean that it will be necessary to add a whole new dimension to your endeavors that might include other associates or an employee to take over what has become routine for you while you venture into new things.

Keeping your confidence and motivation are crucial tasks for the home-based professional so accustomed to external stimulation. There is nothing inherent in the home oriented business that says you have to endure "homeaphobic" encounters with yourself, but there is the added burden of accurate self-diagnosis leading to a productive cure instead of an unwarranted return to the traditional workplace.

• *Rituals.* When routines persist beyond their original useful purposes, they become rituals. Routines in the home office get things done, including your less-than-favorite tasks. Rituals steal time and energy in the name of "we've always done that" behaviors that can rob you of productivity.

Start-up operations at home usually resemble some combination of your traditional office and Saturday-mornings-at-home routines. One of the great satisfactions of home-based employment is this blending of your private and working worlds.

What you must guard against are temptations to let your home business become predominantly an expression of lifestyle, to the exclusion of business image and necessity. If the routines are not proving to be productive, be ruthless enough to break them before they become institutionalized as rituals.

These problems can flow in either direction. Rituals can be rigid business procedures that become destructive to normal relationships in your home—the operation of noisy equipment when others are home that could just as easily be done after they leave. Or they can stem from personal accommodations—like extended morning coffee sessions—that keep you from the business necessities of the day.

Solutions take the form of positive and ever changing adaptations to the realities of both your business and personal obligations. There is plenty of room for each to flourish in the expanded hours of your home-based center of operations, but it takes will to recognize, acknowledge, and change undesirable patterns that threaten to turn desirable individuality into destructive routine.

• *Concentration problems.* The traditional office has its distractions, but they are usually job related. The home office can be surrounded with subtle pressures that beckon you to spend business time in social activities. This is why barriers have to be built, psychological and social, between the residence and the home office. There is a mind set that must be adopted if the home-based professional expects to concentrate on the business at hand and overcome the uneasy guilt of not participating in the normal social discourse of the residence.

Concentration takes on a new meaning in the context of the home working professional. What used to be mere focus on tasks is now active, scheduled avoidance of what would normally be desirable interaction in the setting that once had no internal social boundaries. The home is now two separate environments with different kinds of behavior expected and necessary. It takes concentration and discipline to keep the lines drawn in the expected mode for each.

On the positive side, the home office, properly established, can be a personalized environment that is highly conducive to concentration. Traditional distractions can be screened from your home in ways that would never be acceptable in the corporate setting. Short of someone physically seeking you out, there is no need to receive outside calls during time blocks that you designate prime time. Additionally, there are intangible enhancements to creative thought in the constant and comfortable environment of the home office—fatigue and irritation from the commute and a host of other indirect irritants should be lifted from your shoulders there and concentration enhanced.

• *Sound of silence.* A plus for most people, silence is something to be cherished or, at best, modified at the home office by introducing only your favorite kinds of noise. But there is a disruptive form of silence that can actually interfere with your home-based productivity, if it isn't anticipated and managed.

Individuals have different levels of tolerance for outside stimulation. Silence is a rarity, if it exists at all, but selected audible stimulation—or the lack of it—can help or hinder a person's ability to perform.

Whether your personal choice is a rolling surf and sea birds, or heavy metal, you may work better with music or some background sound. Don't overlook this important element in the psychological atmosphere that you are at liberty to craft in your own image at the home office—other members of the household and neighborhood considered, of course.

• *Need for social mirrors.* There is a requirement for self-evaluation in all our lives and we typically receive a lot of fine tuning in the working environment. Good and bad, the feedback that we receive leads us to lessen our objectionable traits and it strengthens the things we are doing correctly.

The privacy and limited exposure of the home office calls for special compensating behavior in this area of socialization. Few home businesspersons will take to the proverbial mountaintop and forego the need for successful interaction with others. Rather, the home-based professional makes forays into the world for the purpose of influencing clients and others favorably.

Sensitivity may be needed to maintain enough of those know-you-well-enough-to-be-constructively-critical relationships to benefit from life's essential fine tuning. These can take the form of both personal and professional criticism and they are equally important.

Success in business usually parallels successful social interaction with those who constitute your client and peer populations. While a certain amount of mirroring will occur in any active business exchange, you will be wise to remain attuned to the need for seeing yourself in the eyes of these groups.

• *Maintaining perspective.* It is great to be an independent businessperson with an office at home that reflects your own unique needs and tastes—a privilege not enjoyed by the bulk of the workforce. Relish your independence and thrive on the tremendous freedom than you have been able to achieve, but keep the ability to appreciate what it is like on the traditional side of the fence.

Whether you are a management consultant examining the inner workings of a company's underperforming division, or an executive recruiter approaching clients by telephone in the course of their busy days, it needs to be within the context of a fellow professional functioning in the real world. That remains true even after you have been able to eliminate many of the negatives of that world from your own working life.

Perspective can ebb away as you craft your own environment that no longer exposes you to some of the hassle of the normal world of work. Keep in mind that you will still be dependent on the problems of that world and its inhabitants as the grist for your home-based mill. It will be necessary to relate accurately to their situation. You can do so by a carefully managed blend of drawing on past experience and continued immersion on a selective basis.

• *Keeping and enhancing your identity.* To maintain your personal value and your attractiveness to clients, it must always be obvious that you are someone special. Authority should be established while being a member of the traditional team has to be maintained and further developed within your independent identity of a home-based professional.

There is no substitute for reputation and image as an independent operator. Your home-base can contribute quite positively to both, if it is managed and applied correctly. Whether it is a stylish studio or a staid executive office, your home place of business can do a great deal to establish and project your image as someone outside the establishment who can bring clients a special perspective.

Identity is something that you have to internalize before you can hope to convey it to others. By the time you launch your home-based business you will probably have experienced discomfort with what you have become in the traditional workplace. It is generally more than convenience and privacy that pushes professionals to strike out on their own. An overriding consideration is the urge to craft a self-image that more nearly fulfills your most closely held impression of what a successful you looks like.

As an independent home-based worker, you have to establish your own reward mechanisms. Your identity will shift from the image of an establishment company with its logo, dress code, predecessors in your position, and all that goes with the particular corporate look. Enjoy the rewards of establishing a highly personal identity of your own, but expect to earn it with deliberate effort focused on creating the client perceptions needed to warrant confidence and respect.

THE ON-GOING BALANCING ACT

It is evident from the examples discussed that there is a fine line between the stimulating freedoms enjoyed by the home-based businessperson and the seeds of self-destruction. One person's glow of satisfaction individually derived from a highly independent working style can be another's source of torment.

Freedom from the obligations and constraints of life's established patterns can be at once invigorating and threatening. Some find the transition to near total self-management a natural extension of their growth that is highly rewarding. It really can open new vistas of self-satisfaction. The ultimate home-based business experience is to have personal and professional lives blend with such comfort that they become one. The trick to achieving this is perceptive reading of the signs calling for adjustments. This skill will let you reach the point at which both worlds are intact. You will be the richer for the merging.

If you are unsure about the affects of going cold turkey on the traditional workplace, don't pull the plug all at once. Home-based businesses can take many forms, including part-time approaches that let you keep one foot in both worlds for as long as necessary. The next chapter tells you what the combinations are and how they can serve the purposes of the aspiring home-based professional.

Chapter 4

Telecommuter or Entrepreneur?

Millions of people make a living from home-based business activities. Their working arrangements vary widely to embrace an extremely broad range of personal and professional objectives.

- A part-time field editor on the payroll of a national magazine submits her finished story by modem to the main office computer, with photos to follow by overnight mail.
- A full-time, self-employed consultant completes a sophisticated analysis on his own computer and conveys recommendations to client plant managers via fax and a follow-up conference call.

Both are representative of the contemporary home-based worker, although they are at opposite ends of the continuum. One is on payroll—a *telecommuter*, the other self-employed—an *entrepreneur*. One works full time, the other less. What they share is independence from the traditional workplace and the fact that they operate out of home offices.

Taking advantage of the expanding market for expert services and the technology available to deliver it, the most limited business idea can be given a place to take root and grow from a home office. The same is true of the most ambitious scheme. Either can be structured with a mix of workstyle choices that are uniquely your own. An attractive part of the cycle is the ease of transition from one mix to another as client demands and personal objectives are accommodated.

Modern home-based professionals are giving the work-at-home concept a whole new image and definition. These most recent arrivals on the cottage industry scene are thriving because they have positioned themselves favorably within the world of things profitably done with the popularly priced, user friendly technology of the information processing revolution.

YOUR FIRST DECISION

Choose the general approach that you will use to employ the new capabilities in your home-based business. You will find yourself on one side or the other of two basic practices:

1. *Technology based activities.* Performing a task whose objective is the exploitation of the technology itself. Examples include researching electronic databases, accomplishing complex data analyses, doing precision tooling, producing computer art or music, writing applications software, and so on

2. *Technology supported activities.* Operating a conventional business, but with competitive capabilities that would not be possible without technological support. Examples include the executive recruiter, consultant, or marketing professional who ranges the country instead of a limited territory using long distance telephone, fast response fax, and laser printed correspondence to match the finest competitors.

With your initial approach defined, you are ready to select the business to which it will be applied. The next step is deciding the degree of commitment you wish to make.

MIXING AND MATCHING THE POSSIBILITIES

One attraction of the home-based business is its utter flexibility. Before it is discussed fully, look at the work-at-home matrix in Figure 4–1 and see how you might fit your business concept into a workable position in your overall lifestyle. Next look at the possibilities of how it might evolve, depending on your own ambitions and desires. Remember the

	Telecommuter		Entrepreneur	
	Job Related	Not Job Related	Job Related	Not Job Related
Full Time	1	2	3	4
Part Time	5	6	7	8

Figure 4-1 The work-at-home matrix. The numbers in the table's quadrants correspond to cases discussed.

basic difference in orientation between the *telecommuter* and the *entrepreneur*—the former works for someone else as an employee, the latter is self-employed. Both work at home. As you can see, there are a lot of ways to approach home-based work.

- *Case 1: Telecommuter/job related/full time.* If you convince your present firm that your job can be done at home, they keep you on the payroll, but no longer provide you with office space on a day-to-day basis. It involves no disruption in pay or benefits. You have the burden of remaining impressively productive and a necessary part of the team, without being there to interact personally.

- *Case 2: Telecommuter/not job related/full time.* You have found a company that will pay you to perform a service they value while working at your home. It may very well be based on skills you learned in your full-time profession, but it didn't amount to jumping ship to do the same job. This might occur when your employer is too rigid to meet your proposal as a Case 1 worker and you persist until you find someone with somewhat different needs who will accommodate your desired work style.

- *Case 3: Entrepreneur/job related/full time.* You have made the decision that you can do well on your own. The paycheck and benefits will now come from your own home-based business. It is possible either to start at this point or transition to it—usually from Case 1, 5, or 7.

- *Case 4: Entrepreneur/not job related/full time.* Here you have left your regular position and defined some independent course of action that is not a direct application of your primary skills. An engineer or accountant might decide the grass is greener as an independent, specialized executive recruiter, for example.

- *Case 5: Telecommuter/job related/part time.* You may decide that the best way to begin is to maintain a steady income and some of the professional ties available through your old employer. Assuming they really need your skills, it wouldn't be unreasonable to structure an arrangement where you continue to produce for them something they highly value, but do it from home on a part-time basis. Just as possible would be splitting your time between two or more firms who need your services, but not on a full-time basis.

- *Case 6: Telecommuter/not job related/part time.* Frustrated with your career choice, you have received an offer to try something totally different for another firm that sees potential in your abilities and welcomes your offer to try it from home on a part-time basis. You might do this while maintaining your regular full-time position, or let it be part of a full-time home business you have fashioned by adding other part-time endeavors.

- *Case 7: Entrepreneur/job related/part time.* It is always possible to take your mainline profession, fraction it as you please, and market your talents on a part-time basis. Your present employer might or might not be a buyer of your limited services offered from home. If not, you will have identified others who will pay for your input under such an arrangement.

- *Case 8: Entrepreneur/not job related/part time.* You have taken to the home office as an independent practitioner in a field removed from your primary occupation. This can be done as a moonlighting venture in preparation for a mid-life career change in which you want to prove the viability of your business concept before leaving the traditional workplace.

This is not an exhaustive list of all the possible ways to enter or maneuver within the ranks of the home-based worker. It should be comprehensive enough, however, to demonstrate how flexible this way of establishing and conducting a business can be.

DIFFERENT PATHS
TOWARD DIFFERENT ENDS

Some people have the goal of being their own boss and leaving organizational life behind. They want to stay small and specialized. There is no desire to build their own team and risk re-creating the headaches they struggled to leave. Others want to get out there and structure another Apple Computer, Inc., starting in their garage and going on to employ thousands.

For some, the creation of an ego satisfying private enterprise makes the original full-time professional career the more bearable. The original sometimes becomes an enjoyable "sideline" at which the entrepreneur is very good, finds too lucrative and satisfying to give up, and continues to enjoy long after it is needed to make ends meet. Regardless of which model matches your goal, consideration of the operating possibilities begins in the matrix (Figure 4–1).

EXAMPLES OF MAKING IT A REALITY

There are many approaches to structuring your ideal work-at-home situation. Here are a few of them and the steps involved in setting them up:

1. Telecommuter, but in your own home
   - Talk your company into letting you take your computer home and do your work from there several days a week.
   - After demonstrating the viability of the concept, do all of your work at home—making periodic office visits to stay in touch.
   - Make contact with a firm known to use your skills and suggest a part-time work-at-home arrangement after your regular hours—don't overlook the possibility of working across time zones to open up more hours in your day.
   - Solicit a full-time position with a firm known to value your special skills.

2. Entrepreneur, working at home
   - Become an independent contractor and offer your services to your employer on a full-time basis.
   - Using the independent contractor arrangement, make your talents available to several firms from your home-based operation.
   - Establish a conventional business or professional practice from your home office.

3. Telecommuter or traditional/entrepreneur combination
   - Create an acceptably nonconflicting application of your employed skills and market it via your own home-based company —while retaining your outside position (in a traditional setting or as a telecommuter)
   - Keep your job and start a home-based business that gives you the freedom of operation and variety you seek—perhaps in a field far removed from your employed specialty
   - Retain your employed position by choice, after establishing a successful home-based business.

There is a nearly unlimited number of ways to approach the working at home concept. It is up to you to determine where to begin and at what pace you wish to close in on your ultimate objective, assuming it is something beyond your starting point, which could in itself be a worthy goal.

TRANSITIONING YOUR WAY TO THE TOP

Beginning in one mode of home-based enterprise rarely means staying there. It is just too tempting to grow as you refine your business model, accumulate capital, experience, and the client base that beckons you to the next level of commitment. Here are a few illustrations of how the process might unfold for the typical manager or professional:

- *Part-time start up.* Home-based professionals often find themselves testing the waters on an idea they have had, but never implemented. If you find yourself in that situation, you may want to begin your business in the safe harbor of the part-time entrepreneur. Doing so affords you the continued luxury of the full-time position that has been the basis for your lifestyle, credit, and professional identity.

There is no need to disturb what you already have in place. Little real difference will be apparent to the outside world if your den and garage become the flagship office and the shipping center for Jones, Inc.—the new marketing sensation that, through aggressive national telemarketing, is suddenly supplying laser printer and copying machine cartridges overnight at a fraction of the small town suppliers' price! You are a viable player in that market because you have access to the product, the phone to ask for the sale, and the computer to manage the inventory, shipping, billing, and even your calling schedules. Who among your customers knows or cares that you are a part-timer at home if they receive your call when they need a cartridge and you provide it quickly and cheaply—thanks in part to your low overhead home-based business?

• *Part-time/too busy to stay that way.* The start up has matured to the point where it calls for more attention. The answering machine with the half hour tape just isn't doing the job anymore—you are ready for a human order taker or one of the automated order taking systems that can sit in the den twenty-four hours a day, everyday, and, with a Touch Tone® telephone, walk your customers though a telephone order with more efficiency than many operators.

This example is illustrative, but your "product" could just as well be a higher capacity color separation device to support the increasingly sophisticated work your computer graphics shop is doing for its growing list of clients. The point is home-based businesses grow and the means exist to expand them incrementally. It may or may not be time to hire staff or take the plunge into the full-time arena. There are many ways to stretch the time line using various combinations of technology and nontraditional employees attracted to the unique flexibilities of their home-based *employer*—which include, of course, the possible option of working for you at *their* home.

• *Part-time owner/full-time staff.* One way to cope with the growing home-based business that needs more hands, but remains within your ability to manage, is to build full-time staff and keep *your* part-time status. Reasons for doing so could include everything from the fact that you've discovered that you really would miss your regular employment situation to the possibility that the salary from your established employer makes your lenders sleep better.

As a part-time owner with a full-time staff, you enjoy the benefits of both worlds. The situation can be a perpetual one, if you find it satisfying. You won't be the first person to discover that proper delegation of authority by a really capable owner/manager can yield a happy and productive organization benefiting everyone involved. In your own business, there is no requirement that your days be of a certain length, so part-time can really be nearly full-time in terms of effectiveness.

• *Full-time owner/part-time staff.* A logical extension of the "Part-time/too busy to stay that way" model just discussed is for the owner to go full time. Concentrating on managing and marketing the business on a full-time basis, the home-based owner now looks to part time staff to pick up the extra work generated. That could range from neighborhood clerical support, to sophisticated independent contractors helping you to carry the technical work load—even going well beyond your personal technical capabilities, but satisfying contracts that you and your home business have secured.

• *Full-time owner/full-time staff.* This is the full commitment home-based enterprise that can range in size from two people to a substantial staff, limited only by the capacity of your home. One way around the capacity problem is hiring people to work for you from their homes. If your business lends itself to that kind of expansion, the growth possibilities are nearly unlimited. Eliza Collins reported one highly successful computer consulting firm that did just that. Starting in 1962, F International now employees over 1000 freelance workers (Harvard Business Review, 1986).

• *Home office/supporting operation elsewhere.* Finally, the home office can be your executive suite, or nerve center, and the hands on activity can be going on elsewhere. It can take many forms: a desktop publisher might have others with compatible equipment operating from their own homes; a mail order company could be using a "fulfillment house" or "drop ship" arrangement where the warehousing and shipping of orders are handled off-site; a precision milling specialist may be affiliated with a local machine shop that actually does the work using programs he prepares to satisfy orders he acquires.

ABOUT TELECOMMUTING

While the success stories in the home-based business segment come from the entrepreneurial side of the equation, telecommuting can be a valuable transitioning device to that kind of success. It is worth looking briefly at what is going on among the telecommuting employees of hundreds of companies and agencies.

Savage (1988) reports that California has undertaken a program that will put several hundred employees from 11 state agencies on a telecommuting schedule. The hope is that as much as 10 percent of the state's workforce can spend 2 to 4 days a week working out of their homes, saving the state $25 million a year in office leases. Between 500 and 1000 employees at Pacific Bell are in a similar program. Other major firms who employ the concept with growing satisfaction and commitment include J.C. Penny and several major insurance companies.

Marcia Kelly (1986) says that according to the Work In America Institute, one in 5 employees already has an alternative workstyle and that by 1990, 25 percent will have a flexible work schedule. Employers are finding telecommuting necessary and desirable for reasons such as these:

- Increased productivity
- Recruiting advantages
- Increased employee satisfaction
- Increased employee retention
- Increased staffing flexibility and cost control
- Reduced office space requirements.

For the employee, she cites the following attractions:

- Fewer work interruptions
- Increased sense of control over work
- Increased scheduling flexibility
- Savings on food, clothes, and transportation.

The studies and articles stress the necessity of having a well-conceived program supported by top management. There are problems such as the threat to the role of some middle managers when their empires become less visible. People who can work independently are obviously required. The movement is growing, but not as fast as was predicted.

If your goal is to end up with a home-based business of your own, this chapter shows you how to capitalize on some telecommuting arrangements along the way. Part-time telecommuters working for several different client companies can create a situation that can look very much like a business. If you take advantage of the independent contractor status discussed in Chapter 10, you can easily transition to home-based business entrepreneur and hardly know the difference, except in the freedom you enjoy to fashion your professional life.

Chapter 5

Planning and Furnishing a Home Office

As children, we wanted a space of our own. If we had siblings, we longed for the day when the family would move to a larger house or an older brother would leave so we could have our own room. There is something almost sacred about personal space. Psychologists have studied it and found that it is an important factor in our socialization. It is different in other cultures and within the various strata of our own society. Our space, where it is located, and how it is configured is a large component of our satisfaction and happiness.

Living and working spaces, like the human beings who occupy them, have grown in both size and complexity over the generations. The common shelter/workplace of our early ancestors evolved into a series of specialized outbuildings to accommodate increasingly diverse tasks that could no longer co-exist with day-to-day living. Today we have come full circle and the tasks, while complex, are largely clean, cognitive ones that lend themselves to a place in the home again.

Combine these concepts and you have the trend that finds a significant and growing segment of our workforce carving out highly individualized personal work spaces at home. This is in contrast to the broader society's movement to consolidated centers of population and economic activity. The dominance of the common workplace remains a reality that will not change for many workers. For others who depend less on centralized, common capital equipment or traditional work environments, the way is clear to merge the childhood dream of personal space with the adult longing for the ultimately individualized workplace—the home office.

PLANNING YOUR WORKPLACE

The starting point for designing your ideal personal office should be a critical look at all the employer dictated spaces you have occupied over your working life. Such an analysis becomes an informal personality test. Like many psychological inventories, it may reveal little that you didn't already know about your personal likes and dislikes. What it *will* yield is a tangible list of important considerations that you want to respect as you design your perfect home office. Some aspects to consider are discussed next.

Privacy

Some people work best in solitude; others thrive on the din of the busy world around them. In establishing your home office, it is possible to respect such differences. For example, you might situate yourself in a refurbished attic with a dormer window that overlooks a park or distant urban scene—removed from the rest of the household. Or the choice might be a modified guestroom closer to the heart of your home—facing a busy thoroughfare complete with traffic, people at bus stops, deliveries being made, pay phones being used, stores with parking lots and all that go with them. The difference in tone can be quite dramatic within the same residence. You should consider the impact, if it matters to you.

Don't forget to respect the business necessity for home office privacy. It will be essential that you position yourself in such a way as to be free of direct, nonproductive distractions. You will need to escape the routine of the household and avoid disrupting the necessary activities of the other members of the home.

Certain expectations of the traditional business environment will follow you to your home office. Even if you plan to receive few, if any, clients or associates, you will be conducting other business activities such as making and receiving telephone calls. Your compromise with the privacy question will at the very least have to leave you with a businesslike atmosphere for the calls and activities that do expose you to the outside world. No crying children, barking dogs, or grinding garbage disposals.

Some will choose to work side-by-side with a spouse in a shared workspace. Others find it more productive to go to opposite ends of the house. You may face the dilemma of being someone who works best alone or, alternatively, being one who cannot function beyond the sight and sound of another human being. There are ways to solve such problems, if you are aware of their existence and importance. Such personal choices need to be thought through before the first piece of furniture is moved or paint chip examined for your home-based office.

Acoustical Environment

Employer provided offices are always a compromise in terms of what you will be able to hear—or avoid hearing. At the home office, you can more nearly have it your way once you know what "your way" is. Some people cannot think unless they are listening to music. Others need virtual silence in order to engage the brain. While often discussed lightly, both situations can be bona fide productivity factors for the individuals involved.

The home office provides the magic of personal choice. For example, if you work better to the high volume strains of some nonbusiness audio background, be it the soaps or country music, there is a way to listen and not risk offending business callers. Electronic gadgetry shops and catalogs sell a small device that will turn the offensive sound down automatically when you pick up the telephone! Regardless of your choice—nature sounds, elevator music, or hard rock—sound is an important component of the working environment and you can do a lot in the way of optimizing your happiness and productivity if you include it in your home office planning.

Another consideration in sound control is the impact of your activities on others in the household or—worse—the neighborhood or apartment building. If your work centers around an activity that generates sound—a musician, composer, video producer, sound technician, or even a manufacturing function of some kind—remember to consider what you may be doing to others within hearing range. Whether it is a rental lease, a condominium agreement, or a neighborhood zoning law, there is probably something that says you constitute a nuisance and should be put out of business if you fail to cease and desist. The cure may be as simple as a set of headphones or as complex as including sound deadening materials in the design of your home-based business space.

Visual and Lighting Considerations

People have different reactions to what constitutes a favorable lighting environment for them. It doesn't necessarily follow that your ideal complements your optimal productivity. The resulting balance between aesthetic and practical considerations should be incorporated in the design of your home office.

Banks of fluorescent ceiling lights may have a negative connotation for you after a number of years in a commercial office environment. If that is true, don't let that unfavorable association follow you home to your personal office space. There is a tendency to clone the traditional office at home, especially if you are building in a previously unfinished space such as an attic, a basement, or a garage. Avoid the temptation to replicate the visual and lighting atmosphere of the old space in the new, unless it is carry over that you find necessary or desirable.

Everyone doesn't have the luxury of setting themselves up in an alpine chalet, a cottage at the shore, or in a condo 28 stories above Lake Michigan. If you do, by all means capitalize on your good fortune and enjoy the obvious visual pleasures that attracted you in the first place.

If you find yourself in a more traditional residential situation, recall some of the things you always wanted to do to compensate for the shortcomings of the offices you occupied. What would you have done if the building engineer hadn't imposed limitations for the greater good of the group working environment? Modifications of your old plans might work perfectly at home where their impact on the operation of a large commercial space are not a factor.

Air Quality, Ventilation, and Temperature

Emotional exchanges about the rights of smokers and breathers at the traditional workplace are a thing of the past behind the doors of your home-based business. One more personal choice that is yours to make at the home office.

It may have been necessary to wear a sweater in the summer to avoid discomfort from the office air conditioning, or in winter to cope with the energy efficiency plan of your commercial building. The thermostat (and the bill it generates) are under your control at home. Spring and fall now offer the opportunity to open a window and savor the soft, fresh breezes of the changing seasons. Remember that these things are important to you as you choose whether to opt for the increased square footage available in the underground basement or the more cramped, but airy attic with a lofty window.

Mechanically there are ways to cope with almost any physical situation, but it may not be necessary to engineer a solution to your temperature, air quality, and ventilation needs, if the right choices are made to begin with. The place to start is with an inventory of your experiences and preferences compared with the choices before you in your home working space.

Aesthetics

There are regimented offices where periodic inspections see to it that workspaces conform to a master plan of someone's idea of good taste. There are free form offices where each space is a study in the personality and lifestyle of its occupant—not always a pretty sight. You escape having to tolerate either extreme when you establish your own atmosphere at home.

What is pleasing to you is what matters in your space. There are considerations of professional atmosphere for the clients and associates, if you have such an operation. Generally, the charm of the home-based business office is its aesthetic reflection of the occupant. The graphic designer's unfinished loft ceiling contrast nicely with the row of modern flat-files filled with her work. Or the attorney whose vertical blinds and glass fronted bookcases bring a desirable air of the corporate office to his home work area. There is no need to be type-cast when designing your home office. No rules demand that you have walnut paneling when bleached oak or some bright lacquered wood might better suit your personal tastes. Figure 5-1 shows what can be achieved when your tastes and budget allow you to create a professional office at home. Figure 5-2 illustrates how a nicely appointed home office can contain furnishings that let it easily convert into a guest bedroom. Figure 5-3 portrays a functional home office that can be configured with a very modest budget.

Figure 5-1 An elegant home professional office. (© Copyright 1989, Spiegel, Inc.)

Layout

The physical layout of your office at home depends on the amount and configuration of the available space. Unless you are constructing an addition or building out unfinished space, your challenge will be to arrange everything you must do in an efficient way. That will call for aesthetic balance and respect for such things as your budget and other functions that must continue to share the adjacent space.

Figure 5–2 A home office/guest bedroom conversion. (© Copyright 1989, Spiegel, Inc.)

Don't overlook the experience you have from time spent working in other people's environments. Some of the functional standards of the commercial office space can be readily adapted to the home with changes of scale, material, and taste that make them just what you needed. Conversely, remembering the costly wall lights that were more for the designer's satisfaction than the workers' comfort might steer you away from a similar mistake as you consider the layout of track lights and other fixed aspects of your office plan.

One solution to the layout problem is moveable furnishings. Consider commercial or custom built work units that are on casters or locking wheels that can let you transform your space into different configurations as your mood and requirements demand. Another option is the wall unit. It comes in individually priced separate components that can be stacked and arranged to meet your needs. Figure 5–4 shows how a wall unit can be configured to accommodate your basic home office needs.

Figure 5–3 An economical and functional home office. (© Copyright 1988, IKEA, Incorporated)

Checklist of Factors You Control

As you proceed with your home office planning, make a checklist of the factors that you can control. Arrange them as shown in Figure 5–5 on p. 62. The objective is to make note of what is important to *you*. Think of all your pet peeves from offices past and add them to your list of desired accommodations. It may not be possible to achieve them all, but list them *all* and use some judgment as to their relative importance; you should be in a good position to make the best of the choices available in your own particular set of circumstances.

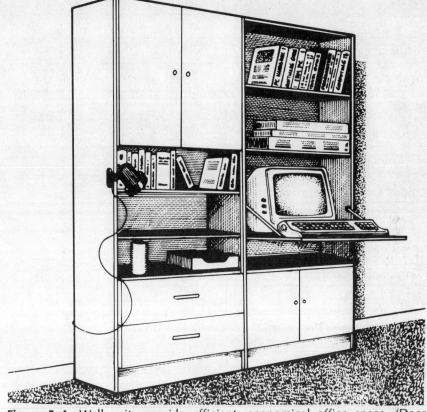

Figure 5–4 Wall units provide efficient, economical office space. (Door Store, Washington, DC and Door Store, Florida)

Don't try to compile your list all at once. Let it evolve over time as you make your plans and become aware of the options available.

WHERE WILL YOU FIND THE SPACE?

Your residence probably contains some underutilized or totally wasted space. Whether it is a mid-town efficiency apartment or a rambling farmhouse a hundred miles away, you can find the necessary space and turn it into an office that reflects much of what you have always wanted and needed in a place to work.

Where do you begin? First take a good look at what you like and dislike in the offices with which you are already familiar. You may not

Factor	Unimportant			Very Important	
	1	2	3	4	5
Artificial lighting					
Fresh air					
Music					
Natural light					
Nonsmoking					
People's company					
Privacy					
Quiet					
Temperature control					
View					

Figure 5–5   Factor Checklist.

get all of the things you want, but you may be pleasantly surprised at how close you can come. Your choices are going to vary widely on the continuum of the efficiency apartment to farmhouse, but even in the smallest of spaces, there are choices to make and situations to optimize.

In "Working at Home," the editors of Better Homes and Gardens (pp. 24–25) suggest that you search your house for possible home office space. Sunset's Home Offices & Workspaces (1986, pp. 40–42) suggests much the same thing with its own emphasis and style. In exploded views of typical residences, the book illustrates possibilities that await in some obvious, and not so obvious, quarters. Here is a list of possible work spaces:

- A room divider, shelving, and a desk might allow you to partition a useful space from an existing living room.
- Wall space in any room could accommodate a specialized unit designed to provide organized space for efficient working.
- A closet can be modified to hold everything you need in an out-of-the-way space, with or without the doors.

- Kitchens have counters, cabinets, and wall space that can be converted into organized office space.

- Attic and basement spaces may take additional effort to convert, but the privacy and space may make them worth the effort.

- An attached garage is an additional room just waiting to be finished.

- Free-standing additions and outbuildings have tremendous potential and can help you to satisfy the tax authorities when they ask for convincing evidence of exclusive business use.

- A bay window, dormer, or other "bump-out" might provide just the extra space needed for your desk and supporting systems.

- Porch or patio enclosures can also provide office space.

- Beneath a staircase or at the upstairs landing, there may be room for the set-up you need.

- Guest rooms can become primary use offices, while retaining their periodic role as visitor's quarters.

This list is not exhaustive and its applicability is limited by the type of dwelling you occupy, but it emphasizes that there are a lot of options to consider when looking for a place to hang your shingle at home. Combine your planning with an awareness of what can be done with unitized office furniture and wall units scaled to residential spaces. Check the specialty catalogs available from major retailers and home furnishing chains. Urban areas have stores that cater exclusively to apartment dwellers trying to optimize the use of limited space. The same items can be useful in a traditional residence where the layout is being modified to accommodate additional functions such as a home office. You may have to approach the problem of gaining more space in the guest room, for example, by looking for unique hideaway bedding more commonly used in efficiency apartments.

A FEW TECHNICAL POINTS TO CONSIDER

Ergonomics

Manufacturers are attempting to design furniture and equipment so that it will be comfortable for the user. The term *ergonomics* is applied to everything from jet fighters to typists' chairs and you have to be the judge of what works for you.

Here is an ergonomic view of what your home computer work station should consist of according to the editors of Sunset's *Home Offices & Workspaces*, (1986, p. 38) who suggest that you should have:

- Seating that keeps your back and neck straight
- Support for the small of your back
- A wrist rest
- No glare
- A document stand the same height as the computer screen
- A keyboard 24 to 27 inches from the floor (lower than your desk)
- Unrestricted leg room (minimum 24" kick space)
- Screen viewing angle of 10 to 30 degrees below eye level and
- Screen located 16 to 28 inches away from your eyes.

Furniture designed to help you meet these guidelines is available from any number of sources. The illustrations in Figure 5-6 are reprinted with permission from The Walker Company, one of many firms who manufacture specialized furniture designed to make your home office comfortable and efficient.

Lighting

A major factor in your working comfort and efficiency is having correct lighting. The following guidelines are adapted from information contained in *The Light Book: A Guide for Lighting Your Home* (1988, pp. 13–14), a General Electric publication.

- *Work area.* The best location is against a plain, light colored, nonglossy wall. Utilize daylight by placing the desk at right angles to a window, but never facing it.
- *Desk lamp.* A desk lamp with the bottom of the shade 15 inches above the work surface, using a low brightness shade with a white or near white lining and one of the following bulb selections. For prolonged use: Soft White 250W; Three Way 80/250W; Multiple Socket 2- 100W. For casual use: Soft White 150W, 170W; Three

MAC MASTER

A full-featured fine oak Macintosh work station that is fully adjustable to provide maximum comfort and productivity for all your computing tasks. A unique tilting mechanism allows the work surface to be adjusted from the horizontal position for normal keying to a 20 degree angle for Cad/Cam and desktop publishing. The work surface automatically tilts as it is effortlessly pulled out from its compact horizontal position. Five preset stops insure maximum comfort and productivity. Fully extended, the MacMaster provides a spacious 7.7 square feet of desktop space.

MacMaster also features an adjustable tilt monitor shelf which allows the monitor to be adjusted for maximum comfort and reduced eye strain. Ample room is provided for a second monitor, printer, etc.

- Constructed from the finest grades of hardwood and oak veneers.
- Adjustable tilt monitor(s) shelf.
- 5 position tilting work surface (7.7 square feet).
- Heavy duty twin wheel casters glide easily over carpets.

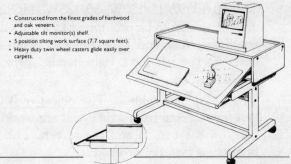

THE WALKER
COMPANY

PC CENTRAL

The elegant executive computer accessory... PC Central. Fine oak, careful design, and traditional craftsmanship are combined to give you a truly practical solution to computer "clutter".

The PC Central organizes your computer, printer and peripherals. At the same time it provides ample room for your mouse, assorted paper work, books, a second monitor, hard drives, etc. In short, PC Central gives you the extra space you need to be more productive.

No need to lose time and thought when called away from your computer, be it ten minutes or a day. Simply slide the keyboard/work surface back into the unit and it's out of the way, undisturbed until you are ready to continue.

Heavy duty casters allow the PC Central to be wheeled across the office or across the hall.

A double width document support allows ample space for multiple documents, books, or folders. Built with an ingenious hinge system, the document support can be easily folded out of the way when not in use.

- Almost 5 square feet (693 square inches) of work space.
- 13.8 square feet of shelf space.
- Heavy duty twin wheel casters glide easily over carpet.
- Finest grades oak hardwood and fine oak veneers. Finished with a durable and easily maintained lacquer finish.
- Available in natural oak or walnut stain to compliment any decor.
- Easily assembled in ten minutes with only a screw driver.

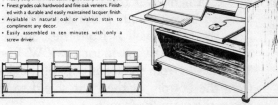

THE WALKER
COMPANY

PC EXECUTIVE

Practical Elegance in Classic Oak

Bring the richness of oak to your computer work center. PC Executive, the practical alternative to steel and plastic laminate. Each piece of the PC Executive line is hand crafted of the finest grades of real oak hardwood and fine oak veneers. Finished with a two step lacquer process, then hand rubbed into a durable finish that will last a lifetime. With the optional drawer, shelf unit and printer cart, the PC Executive becomes the complete executive computer work center. An elegant addition to any executive suite.

- Available in natural oak or walnut stain finish to compliment any decor.
- Sturdy solid oak legs.
- Durable hand rubbed lacquer finish.
- Heavy Duty twin wheel casters glide effortlessly over any carpet.

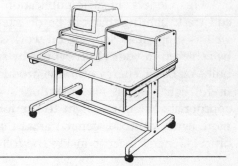

THE WALKER
COMPANY

Figure 5–6 Computer tables designed for comfortable productivity. (The Walker Company, Petaluma, CA)

Way 50/150W, 15/150W, 50/185W; Multiple Socket 2-75W. A desk lamp should be positioned 15 inches to one side of the center of the work and 12 inches back from the front edge of the desk. To the left for a right-handed person, to the right for a left-handed one.

- *Visual display terminals.* The objective is to light the keyboard and the material from which you are working while keeping the light off the person and the screen. The shade can be of low brightness material or opaque.

- *Hanging fixtures.* Should be positioned the same as a desk lamp, 15 inches above the surface. The shade should be of a low brightness material with a white lining, and the bulb recommendations are the same as for the desk lamp.

- *Fluorescent shelf light.* Can provide more space and a wider spread of light over the work area. The light source should be shielded by an opaque material and it should let some light up from the top as well as from the bottom. Tubes recommended are 36 inches-30W or 48 inches-40W. Placement should be 9 to 12 inches in from the front edge of the desk and 15 to 18 inches from the bottom of the light shield to the desk top, centered above the main work area.

This General Electric publication also notes that it is possible to add track lighting that can be directed to create decorator effects as well as supply task lighting on work surfaces. Substantial savings can be achieved in your electrical use by substituting lower watt reflector bulbs or other energy efficient products that yield the same levels of useful light. Age is also mentioned as a factor in determining the appropriate amount of light to use for a given task. Older eyes need more light. In broad, general areas that have relevance for the home office, General Electric makes the following recommendations:

Task	Easy-Short Duration	Critical or Prolonged
Reading	Low to Moderate	High
Study	Moderate	High
Typing, computer	Moderate	High
Writing	Low to Moderate	High
Workbench	Moderate	High

Using the guidance provided in this section, you can avoid unnecessary fatigue, discomfort, and inefficiency in your home office work space.

A MATTER OF PRIORITIES

Whether you are at the point of furnishing an elegant executive home office, or just getting around to replacing the card table in the den with a respectable computer table and chair, you have many options from which to choose. The decorator touch is something you can certainly enjoy when the time comes, but that can wait for the proving years to pass. Spend your start-up time, energy, and resources on establishing a comfortable working office that will meet the combined necessities of your home and work lives within the single residence. Respect the commonsense necessities of privacy, adequate work surfaces, light, and so on. Then quickly be about the business of business. There is nothing more meaningless than the well appointed office of a failed business —few things more incontestable than the character laden surroundings of a successful one.

Chapter 6

Computers and Telecommunications

You and your special talents constitute the *substance* of a viable business and the basis for commanding fees that will provide an independent livelihood. Revolutionary products and services that have come into existence in recent years make it possible for you to do so from a home-based office. This chapter describes a sampling of what is available and suggests ways to choose prudently from the nearly overwhelming array of supporting technologies.

Figure 6-1 illustrates the components likely to make up the technological heart of a typical home-based professional office. Financially, these are well within your reach, the complete home computer configuration would cost about $1500, add another $200 for the telephone/answerer, and you can see that the impressive picture isn't at all beyond the grasp of a home office operator. Shop carefully and you can find the exact configuration for your budget *and* needs from any number of manufacturers and suppliers.

THE "NECESSITIES"

Regardless of what you plan to do as a home-based businessperson, you are going to need certain pieces of equipment. Some would have

Figure 6–1 Affordable technology for the home office. (© Copyright 1989, Spiegel, Inc.)

sounded like luxuries a few years ago, but now they qualify as bedrock necessities for both image and efficiency.

Telephone

No modern dwelling would lack telephone service—no respectable home-based professional would fail to have that vital link to customers and clients meet a few fundamental tests. The telephone needs to be answered every time it rings and in a pleasant, businesslike manner. The line needs to be a private one and, preferably, dedicated to business, that is, one that doesn't risk being treated as a personal convenience by other members of the household. The instrument itself need not be anything special, beyond considerations of clarity, reliability, and user comfort—if it is to be used for extended periods.

Word Processing

Although the modern home-office relies heavily on direct, personal communication by telephone, there is still the need to prepare bids, contracts, reports, and other documents. Although these can be done via an old-fashioned typewriter, once you experience the convenience of modern word processing, it is unlikely that you will settle for less. Being a solo act, you will be all the more attracted to the efficiencies of word processors that check your spelling, lend themselves to easy modification, and more.

The home-office word processor is not a separate piece of equipment, rather it is just one more piece of inexpensive software to add to the computer system you will almost certainly have for bookkeeping, database, or specialized professional support. Properly selected, the products you need can be acquired reasonably and will add priceless efficiency and professional image enhancement to your business. Save

Figure 6-2 A word processing alternative to the personal computer. (© Copyright 1989, Spiegel, Inc.)

the old typewriter for addressing the periodic envelope or completing an occasional form.

If you think that a personal computer is more than you need for your word processing needs, consider one of the popularly priced (about $800 at publication) units dedicated to that task. The model illustrated in Figure 6–2 also has spreadsheet and spelling checker capabilities. Look at this carefully, however, since a word processor as a separate piece of equipment cannot be enhanced. Whereas a computer can do many tasks for you.

SPECIALIZED HOME OFFICE SUPPORT

Once you have established the basic communication links via the telephone and computer generated correspondence, you should take a prudent look at what else might be added that would enhance your operation. Without becoming a technology junkie and devoting more energy to its selection and application than is warranted, have an objective look at what might give you expanded capabilities as you project your services into the markets you have identified.

The first level of specialization would be to up-grade the fundamental equipment that you used to start the business. There is a whole continuum of quality and sophistication that goes with every item you use. Computers, printers, software, telephones, services of every kind —start simple and go into your up-grades with a dual appreciation for what you need and the fact that even better things will be coming on line soon.

Next, you will want to examine the needs of your specialty that justifiably call for more than the basics. If you are a desktop publisher, for example, the computer and supporting printer and software will be substantially more complex than those needed for the consultant more intent on selling data than finished product presentations. If you are an executive recruiter or a telemarketer who spends hours on the telephone, there is specialized equipment that can make you more comfortable and efficient.

The sections that follow will touch upon a variety of choices in home office equipment and service options. Your task as a home-based professional is to pick and choose wisely. False economies that deny you the capabilities to impress your clients with the very best services that you are capable of generating are unwarranted. Excesses that can actually waste valuable working time and financial resources are equally undesirable for the home-based businessperson trying to strike the optimum balance and sustain profitability.

Understanding Your Computer Needs

This overview is a generic approach to the necessary appreciation of computers and all that goes along with their use. If you are already using a desktop computer, this discussion will help you round out your thinking and perhaps identify some things that you've been missing. If the whole field is new to you, it will give you the big picture and the basis for dealing intelligently with those who can help you with the details. The objective is to convey a sense of the capabilities available, the ranges of sophistication that exist, and the appropriate terms used to trigger the desired responses from those who know more than you probably will ever care to.

HOW A COMPUTER SYSTEM WORKS

A personal computer, a desktop computer, a laptop computer, a mini-computer—or whatever the term-of-the-day may be—is nothing more than a glorified television set with the added capacity to store and process information. That's accomplished by an internal *microprocessor* or super-miniaturized set of circuits. To that you add the necessary *internal storage* to let it do a lot of very fast and complex electronic shuffling on the inside while you instruct it and await the results on the outside.

Getting the information in and out requires *disk drives* (turntable-like devices) and *magnetic disks* (record or CD sort of things). You add a typewriter-like *keyboard* for entering data—a *numeric pad,* if you're more at home with a calculator layout—or some other way to communicate the data into and out of the computer. One popular variation: a *modem* that will let you accomplish the necessary communication via telephone. Another is the *scanner*—a device that will turn a picture into an electronic pattern readable by the computer. There are specialized *input* and *output devices* capable of everything from monitoring laboratory experiments to generating musical notation. Not to be overlooked, the most common output device of them all, the *printer.*

Everything discussed so far has been *hardware*—equipment. The other half of the formula is *software*—specialized electronic instructions that make it all work. The latter takes the form of *programs.*

People with more patience (and genius) than I, spent interminable hours devising *languages* with which programmers and developers tell the computer how to take certain actions. Programmers have, in turn, taken the languages and constructed long chains of logical code that result in the computer being able to respond to you.

Programs take one of two forms. There are *systems programs* (MS-DOS and the Macintosh operating systems, for example) that are the intellectual guts of your particular brand of computer. And there are *applications programs* that use the systems just mentioned to go on and accomplish specific tasks—word processing, spreadsheet analysis, tax preparation, database management, flight simulations, or virtually anything you see in the computer magazines and stores.

SELECTING YOUR COMPUTER SYSTEM

Unless you have a burning desire to know more, all you need concern yourself with is selecting the software and hardware required to do the task you have in mind. With few exceptions, you can do that based on your existing knowledge and experience with computers at work. If that is lacking, find a computer literate friend and get their opinion of how you might best proceed. It is often wise to do some personal research in the computer magazines, library, and bookstore. If you are totally new to computers, you might consider hiring a computer consultant (often a home-based professional!) to help you.

Some consumers shop for weeks to select a new TV set or an appliance, others are impulse buyers—computers are rapidly becoming appliances and their buyers reflect these same patterns of behavior. You won't go far wrong in selecting any of the standard packages if you buy from a *reputable* dealer. Your main considerations are:

- Will it run the kinds of software you need?
- Will it support the printer or other equipment you want?
- Does it fit your budget?
- Are you comfortable with its operation?
- Can you easily get it serviced?
- Is there someone to call with an operating question?
- Will it accommodate your expected growth?

The popular computer market is divided into IBM compatible systems and the Apple family now dominated by various levels of the Macintosh line. Strong brand loyalties exist, but the lines are blurring as the best features of both are being adopted by the other and major software producers cater to either operating system. Both have nonprofit users' groups all over the country that can be identified by talking with the local computer dealers or calling the user services number of the manufacturers—hardware or software.

If you are still uncomfortable with buying a home computer system, consider hiring a consultant for a few hours of advice. The Yellow Pages list them, but keep in mind that it is easy to purchase advice exceeding the cost of a packaged system that will both meet your immediate needs and give you the experience on which to base future choices. The other hazard with consultants is getting into levels of sophistication that you really don't need. Make it clear that you are talking about selecting a home computer system and off-the-shelf software, not a custom small business system with individualized programming. If they are still on the line, you may have reached someone who can be helpful.

There is no substitute for actually *using* computer equipment and software to learn what you like. One approach is to consider your first system to be a few thousand dollars well spent in experiential computer education.

A call to the local users' group will also turn up people with no vested interest, beyond their own bias, who would either recommend a consultant or personally volunteer to help you out of the sheer love of sharing their knowledge. Don't overlook the value of having such a contact to call when the damned thing won't do what it obviously should!

The system you ultimately acquire will consist of software that accomplishes the specific task, and hardware to actually do the work—processing the information and producing the necessary output. Software supplies the brains; hardware, the brawn. As you will see, the two cannot really be dealt with separately, even though they form the basic dichotomy that frames all computer terminology discussions.

Software (The Application Programs)

The most natural approach to acquiring a home computer system is to head for the computer store and start looking at the different kinds of hardware available in your price range. For the home-based business person, I recommend beginning at the software end of the system. Your concern is for what tasks the computer will do for you, at what level of sophistication, and how easily. The most understandable literature addressing those points is the advertising and user manuals of the software manufacturers—and the reviews published in the popular computer magazines.

The single best way for the novice to break the code on what is apt to be personally useful is by plunging into the software literature. The overall purpose of the software will be apparent by its advertising and cataloging (word processing, accounting, desktop publishing, etc.). Then proceed to isolate a number of products that sound promising and dig more deeply. Read the magazine reviews. Go to software stores and peruse the user's manuals. *Actually try it on the the store's equipment.* There is no approach to the mystery of home computer capabilities that will be more relevant or easily understood by the novice user —software advertising and manuals speak your language and address your needs. The manual is as important as the program itself. Once the purchase is made, the manual becomes your instructor.

After you have determined which software product has the best balance of necessary features and ease of use, read on and let the software manufacturer tell you what kind of hardware is needed to make it run. You will need to know which operating system is required (there is often a version available for either of the popular operating systems). They will also tell you what capacity your computer must have—the 1 megabyte (Mb) size of the Apple Macintosh Plus, for example, is rapidly becoming the minimum desirable for popular full-function applications. Everything from the old 64K models on up still do a lot of useful things; they just don't have the capacity to allow you to use the newer, more powerful software. The industry has progressed to where the greater capacities are available at little additional cost and the software often requires the greater capacity. You will also be given a recommendation on the type and number of disk drives recommended to get the most from the software.

Plan to legitimately *purchase* the software. Avoid the temptation to break the strict laws against making a copy of the one you use at the office or the version acquired by a friend. There are real benefits to making the purchase. You register with the manufacturer and qualify for inexpensive upgrades as they are developed. A user services telephone number is provided where you can get endless technical assistance on the use of the application for the cost of the telephone calls. The greatest payback for your honesty; however, is the constant flow of bigger and better software products coming to market as a result of the profit incentive you sustain with your purchase.

There is free "public domain" software provided by users' groups and even manufacturers. Another noncommercial avenue is "shareware" programs. You acquire them for a minimal fee to the developer, with the understanding that you will pass it on to others with the same expectation—sort of a software chain letter, but without the negative overtones. These two sources can provide some nice-to-have extras, but your principal home-based business software will be proprietary and should be purchased.

There is single function software designed to accomplish one thing —word processing, for example. Another choice is multiple function or "integrated" software designed to let you flow easily from one application to another. For instance, a popular combination of programs is word processing, a database manager, and communications software. When you buy it, you are assured that all three are compatible and that you can comfortably move a report created in the database into a letter created in the word processor and then send it to someone using your modem and the communications program. The same thing can be accomplished using individual applications, but you will need to take the added trouble of investigating compatibility and possibly buying more software to facilitate working on multiple applications at the same time. Usually, the separate programs are individually more powerful.

Your software choices all come down to the question of what is needed to do the job you have in mind. Do you just want to write simple letters, or would it be worthwhile having the capability to preview the layout on the screen before printing it? How about bold, italics, mixed typefaces, alphabetizing and summing columns? The list goes on and that can be said for most kinds of applications. Start with something simple enough that you will use it freely. If it is too complex, you may avoid it. As familiarity and changing needs warrant, up-grade your software.

One more way to approach the software decision and, indirectly, your hardware selection is to attend a workshop on some popular application. It will be money well spent on learning what the software (and hardware) can do and why you might want to position yourself a notch or so up or down the scale of complexity. It will give you a hands-on benchmark for further exploration and choice.

Hardware (Equipment)

Now that you have tentatively selected your software and have at least identified the minimum hardware required to operate it, you need to sort out some important choices. In our discussion of how a computer system works, we named the essential components. Now it is time to examine each of them more fully.

Computer. Unless regular portability is a requirement (in which case, you will be looking at laptops), you can make do with any of the desktop models. They vary in price and complexity from simple word processors with built-in software, to sophisticated units that can be enhanced to handle almost any function you are likely to need. Capacity and adaptability to changing needs are two of your most important considerations. Unless there are compelling reasons to own the cheapest or the most complex, start somewhere in the broad middle ground of the popular models of the major manufacturers. Go to the dealers and try the different models. Ask to use the software you have in mind. See if they can suggest something better for your purposes and investigate it along with what you had tentatively selected.

Monitor. Your choices in video displays are no longer as simple as they once were, but avoid the temptation to buy more than you need. Some have a higher resolution than others—they have more dots per unit of measure and therefore show more detail. Some are color and others are monochromatic (green, orange, black-and-white)—unless your work requires color, there is no reason to pay for it. The other basic consideration is screen size. Monitors are available in all sizes including special elongated models to display a full length typeset page— ideal for the desktop publisher, a costly extra for the normal user. In the absence of a good reason to do otherwise, the standard monitor that comes with the computer is fine.

Keyboard. The standard keyboard is all most people will ever need. Check to see whether it has a numeric pad, if entering data is going to be a large part of your work—if not, they are sold as inexpensive extras or buy the *enhanced* keyboard. Other than special purpose keyboards useful to programmers and technical specialists, there is little reason to do more than stay away from the cheap, undersized models. Most of the leading computers come with an industry standard full size and feature keyboard.

Disk Drives. Your computer will come with at least one drive and it is increasingly common to have two. For most applications, it is almost essential that you have the second drive. Without it, you will spend a lot of aggravating time swapping disks—the computer will need to switch back and forth frequently between the program that tells it how to perform the task and your working disk that contains your data—it can be maddening. The best solution, and an increasingly affordable one, is the *hard disk*. That is an enclosed metal storage device that holds larger amounts of information and is capable of being easily accessed. The alternative is the *floppy disk*—the kind you carry around and insert in the drives to load your programs and data. They have come a long way—so far, that the floppy is rarely floppy anymore. The more popular version is the 3.5 inch plastic-encased disk that will fit in your shirt pocket and take more abuse than its 5.25-inch soft-sided predecessor. The newer version also holds several times the data (800K) of the old floppy. Hard disks now generally start at 20,000K and are available in 10,000K increments up to very substantial capacities. To give you some appreciation of what these capacities mean, this entire book was written and sent to the publisher on one 800K 3.5 inch floppy disk—and there was room to spare.

Printers. Five kinds of printers may confront you in your search for the one most appropriate to your needs:

- Ink jet printers whose heads actually shoot ink onto the paper; most often found on small, portable printers or plotters, but also available in sophisticated versions that rival the quality and capabilities of expensive laser printers for about the price of the best dot matrix models.

- Thermal printers require a special paper that is sensitive to heat; usually limited to small portables.

- Daisy wheel impact printers, often called "letter quality" because they are essentially typewriters. The main limitation is that they have little or no graphics capabilities and only one typeface can be used at a time—the daisy wheel has to be physically changed.

- Dot matrix printers that have heads consisting of pins that change position to form letters and characters—the more pins, the finer the image formed. They are variously known as "draft quality" (few pins), "near-letter quality" (more pins), and "letter quality" (lots of pins—27 or so). Some have variable settings that allow you to run with the degree of quality needed—the less quality, the faster the words per minute of printing. These are the leading products in the popular printer market because they present a wide range of quality options at a reasonable price. They have the ability to do graphs and artwork. Inexpensive dot matrix printers cost several hundred dollars; medium quality, around $500 to $800; and high quality with features for individual sheet feed, envelope handling, etc. can cost $1,000 and up.

- Laser printers are considered the top of the line in terms of quality and versatility. They use "engines" that are essentially copying machines where a cartridge of fine black plastic powder is attracted to differently charged surfaces on plain paper, then made permanent with heated rollers. As long as the software is in place in the computer and the printer, virtually anything can be printed—mixed typefaces, graphics, half-tone art, and almost anything else you can name. Laser printers spawned the desktop publishing industry, along with special page layout software.

  They are sheet feed and there is no head impacting the paper, so they have two limitations that cause some users to keep a dot matrix for special tasks. Those tasks are running continuous form paper, labels, invoices, and so on and multi-part forms where impact is needed to make the carbon copies. Lasers are rapidly coming down in price and can now be purchased in the $1000 to $5000 popular range with special models running proportionally more.

The printer decision should be based on the kind of work you need to produce. If it is desktop publishing or an artistic application, or you need to produce fancy correspondence using a mix of type faces in a single document, the laser is probably what you want. If you need very good, but not perfect printed documents, a high quality dot matrix or ink jet printer may be satisfactory.

It is important to use care in selecting a printer that is sufficiently "compatible" with your computer and software. Generally, buying the printer of the computer manufacturer solves this problem. There are third party vendor printers that do an outstanding job and meet the compatibility test, but be sure they are compatible with *your* computer. Sometimes special features like italics or bolding just won't work on certain combinations of computers, printers, and software. If possible, actually print sample documents that represent the kinds of formats and features that you will be using—before believing the compatibility claims of the manufacturers.

Modems. Your computer has the potential to receive and send data over telephone lines through a peripheral device known as a modem. The purpose might be to communicate with your home office while on the road, or to participate in a professional or user conference—or do research—on computer information networks like *CompuServe.* The modem is a "blackbox" that turns your computer into something that can speak and be understood via telephone transmission.

Modems come as separate units and as built-in components of hard disks. If separate, you have the ability to upgrade, repair, or replace either device independent of the other. What you may gain by having them together is some increased compactness and portability. There is communications software that comes with the modems and gives them the ability to function. The other big variable is speed of transmitting and receiving. This is expressed in baud rates of 1200, 1800, 2400, and so forth. If you will be using it a lot with information services that charge by the minute, one of the higher speeds may be worth considering, although user rates are somewhat higher for the faster modems. Other options include variations on software and equipment that will let your computer operate after hours without you being present.

Fax Modems. There are also combinations that will let your computer and modem serve as a fax machine of sorts. Browner and Norr (1989) recently concluded that these devices currently have limitations that outweigh their advantages for the average user. They are new on the market and improvements will make them more attractive in the future. For now, they are outstanding for certain kinds of text transmission between computers. The down side is that they have some incompatibilities with other fax machines, some tie up your computer and make it impossible to use for other purposes while sending or receiving fax, and the only way they can handle documents not generated on the computer is by using a supplementary scanner. At this point in their development, the fax modems are probably a less desirable option for the home office than the dedicated fax machines discussed in the telecommunications section of this book.

Backup Devices. It is always possible that something will go wrong with the disk that you have your work stored on, whether a simple floppy or an elaborate hard disk. Without getting into all of the technical possibilities, let us just say that you will be very glad a copy is filed away somewhere else.

There are different ways to make such a backup copy. The simple way is to use the copy feature of your computer and its disk drives to make another copy on floppy disks—one or several, depending on the size of your document. A hard disk with a lot of data on it will require more than one floppy. It can become a sufficiently awkward process that you want to purchase a tape backup system and the software that goes along with it.

For the average user, consideration of more than a floppy disk backup system can wait. The habit of backing up on floppies is absolutely essential. You must develop it from the beginning. Imagine having the great American novel down to the last chapter and your computer cryptically informs you that your disk is no longer readable! It happens, although modern computers and storage media are very reliable. There is also "first aid" software that can do a lot to recover data from damaged disks. The only prudent approach, however, is to "save" regularly as you work and backup at least at the close of each session. The wisdom in the trade is never fail to save or backup more work than you can afford to loose—15 minutes? hours? days? weeks? It's up to you.

Scanners.   Converting images to electronic data streams readable by your computer is the job of the scanner. They come with different capabilities. Some will scan text—typewritten only/print typeface only, all sorts of variations. Others will scan line drawings. Still others will convert photographs and paintings with different levels of sophistication and quality. Black-and-white or color is another option. Unless you are a desktop publisher, you probably will not have an interest in scanners, but you should be aware of their usefulness as an input device for nonartistic applications—they can save a lot of "keyboarding."

Networking Systems.   As your home office grows and more than one computer is involved, you may want to consider having them "talk" to each other and share common peripherals such as printers and backup devices. This is accomplished by networks that physically wire the computers together and network software that manages the resulting system—saying whose job goes to the printer next, and so on. The role of the network is similar to that of the modem and both have to be considered, if you are going to be networking across town or across the country. A term that you might encounter is local area network or LAN. When you reach the point of needing such services, it is time to consider spending some money on a consultant who is proficient in such things.

UNDERSTANDING YOUR TELECOMMUNICATIONS NEEDS

There is much more to consider than the purchase of a telephone system for today's home-based business. The line that enters your home office opens the door to a host of optional services that can link your business to national or even international markets. Wise use of these powerful services can act as a multiplier that gives your home-based enterprise the image and impact of a major player in your field.

Half of the telecommunications formula is the physical devices you select. There used to be a clear distinction between commercial and consumer grade telephone equipment. That line has grown blurred and many of the most sophisticated products are now popularly available and competitively priced. Top-of-the-line consumer grade products are perfectly satisfactory for many home office applications.

Telephones

Telephones are popularly available that will perform any of the tasks you might need in your home office. If your business demands only routine calling, it makes little sense to buy an elaborate, multi-featured set. You may have occasion to call a certain set of numbers frequently —if so, avail yourself of the memory telephones that will do the dialing for you. Executive recruiters, who find themselves straining to hear soft speaking clients, can benefit from a volume control feature. Marketing people can justify the expense of a comfortable headset. Telephones that accommodate a second line are readily available in the retail marketplace now. Last number re-dial is on almost any telephone sold. Speaker phones are handy, but have never overcome the talking-from-the-bottom-of-a-well quality that limits their use to informal, working conversations with friends. Prices are relatively low and you can afford to experiment until you find the combination of features best suited to your home office requirements.

Figure 6-3 illustrates an assortment of popularly marketed telephones and answering machine combinations suitable for the

Figure 6–3 A selection of telephones and answering machines suitable for home office use. (© Copyright 1989, Spiegel, Inc.)

home-based business. Similar models are available from a variety of reliable manufacturers. Prices are in the $100 to $250 range, depending on the number of features associated with the particular unit.

Avoid telephones that are obviously cheap—they sound that way and lessen your professional image. Don't get talked into "expandable" office grade systems that you may never need. They can always be added when you outgrow the perfectly adequate popular models that can get you started economically.

Service is nice, but not a big consideration—most telephones can be replaced about as cheaply as they can be repaired and a lot more quickly. A good local retailer is probably more valuable for his advice than his repair capabilities. He can explain features, order special items, and advise you about all sorts of special items like plugs that will keep summer lightening storms from ruining your equipment.

Figure 6–4 shows some of the futuristic telephones that are available today. The Mitsubishi Visitel™ is a telephone with an added feature of being able to take, store, and transmit freeze frame black-and-white photographs in the course of your telephone conversation. It is available for about $900. The other currently available future phone is a portable cellular that works the same way the popular automobile telephones do except with a weight of 18 ounces it goes with you anywhere. The price at publication is about $1600.

Answering Machines

A mainstay of the home office is the telephone answering machine. The alternative is an answering service, but unless it is a very good one, it won't match the professionalism, reliability, convenience, and economy of a properly used machine. While the features vary widely, they improve constantly; yesterday's luxury is today's standard. As of this writing, the minimum features would be remote paging from a Touch Tone® telephone and the feature that lets you know when there are no messages so you can hang-up and avoid a long distance charge. Other features include digital recording of the outgoing message that puts your voice on a chip that doesn't deteriorate the way a tape does and time/date stamping of messages so you know when your calls were received.

Figure 6–4 Futuristic telephones that are on the market today. (© Copyright 1989, Spiegel, Inc.)

Personalized Voice Systems

While the comparison is simplistic, personalized voice systems are extensions of answering machine technology. Instead of relying on a microchip for their capabilities, these advanced devices are more apt to call upon a dedicated computer to direct their more complex functions. The systems interact by voice with callers who use their telephones to find their areas of interest among its branching information options. Here is a sampling of capabilities available today from Microlog Corporation, a Germantown, Maryland company that specializes in this kind of equipment.

- *VCS 3500 Automated Attendant* serves as an automated receptionist/answering service using a prerecorded greeting and voice prompts that render assistance. A human operator can be a single digit touch away. Such a device can deal with routine calls in an individualized way, breaking through to you or a staff member only when necessary.

- *VCS 3270 Voice Response System* is used for turning the phone into a sophisticated device for accessing your computer data. Customers talk to the computer through Touch Tone® telephone input and are answered in spoken English. It can take orders, give account information, handle money transactions—anything now done by an operator at a keyboard.

- *VCS 3500 Automated Transaction Processing* can process orders without mistakes, get information from clients without missing a point, and give your callers prompt, courteous service all day long. With it, you can get information when it's convenient for your callers and process it when it's convenient for you. It asks a series of questions and records the answers. It can be programmed to take multiple calls and simultaneously provide the requested information. Using a technique called "Intelligent Branching," it can be directed by the caller to disseminate variable information such as business locations, hours of operation, directions, or record caller responses, take orders, complaints or other customer responses. It can even be programmed to deliver different messages in many languages to a variety of audiences.

- *VCS 3500 Automated Outbound Dialing* will deliver selected messages in any combination to hundreds of people by calling them on your behalf.

This brief listing of features was adapted from Microlog's current literature and is intended to start you thinking about the communications power that can be packed into a home office operation. The more sophisticated configurations are not inexpensive, but cost is relative and has to be examined in light of what you are trying to accomplish. A very sophisticated, high quality, high volume calling or response system can be operated from a home office, if you have a business function that will justify this kind of support. For more complete information on what this kind of equipment can do—and its current cost—call Microlog at 800-562-2822 or 301-428-3227.

Fax Machines

The practice of sending hard copy text and photographs with the speed of a telephone call is being viewed by many as the greatest leap in popular commercial technology since the advent of the computer. Figure 6–5 is a compact facsimile machine that will use your current telephone line, transmit a letter in less than a minute, do double duty as a copier, and cost you less than $1000.

Terry Moffatt (1989) makes the point that the fax is becoming a technological standard by which small businesses and independent professionals are being judged. Moffatt's research predicts that by the mid-1990s there will be 20 million users operating close to 4 million fax machines. A very attractive piece of equipment for the home-based professional, he cites the following reasons why:

- Speed: 12 seconds to send a page around the world
- Economy: a $14 overnight delivery service fee from New York to Los Angeles for a 10-page document equates to about $2 by fax
- Price: now available in the $1000 to $3000 price range, down from $3000 to $5000 little more than a year ago
- Ease of use: very simple to operate, as opposed to computer-to-computer arrangements that are faster and more sophisticated, but more difficult to use.

Figure 6–5 A popularly priced fax appropriate for the home office. (© Copyright 1989, Spiegel, Inc.)

The features that you have to choose from in selecting a fax machine are much the same as those available for computer modems, telephone answering machines, and computer printers. Your choices revolve around questions of image quality, unattended use, and automatic dialing features. Many of the newer fax machines also double as limited use copying machines in the home office. Figure 6–6 illustrates how a fax

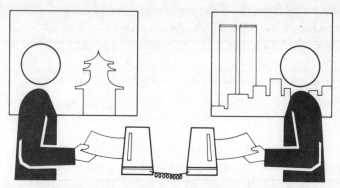

Figure 6–6 Hard copy is now easily sent around the world via fax. (Reprinted with permission of AT&T from *Telecommunications Ideas to Grow On* Series. © 1989 AT&T. All Rights Reserved.)

can put the home-based business operator in nearly instant hard copy communication with the world.

SERVICES

The key to benefiting from the telecommunications revolution is recognizing and using the powerful services of the major suppliers. They were developed and are still primarily supported by huge business organizations that dominate various segments of the economy. Miraculously, they are equally available to the home-based business. You don't have to be an established mail order house with a multi-million dollar customer service budget to deal with your customers as though you were. An excellent selection of printed materials and videos are available from AT&T. Since they often update and produce new materials, call 1-800-533-9782, Extension 6101 and request their latest list.

Telecommunications is now a highly competitive industry. While the examples that follow are based on the products of one vendor, the reader is encouraged to seek comparisons from the many fine companies that market similar products and services.

Telecommunications for the Home-Based Business

There are basic ways in which telecommunications can serve the home-based business. Ideas that follow have been adapted by the author for home office use from the *Telecommunications Ideas to Grow On* series (1986) produced by AT&T. (A 1989 revision will soon be available.) Since the early 1980s, the telecommunications industry has become a competitive one and many of the services mentioned may also be available through other companies listed in your local telephone directory.

Planning

Consultants in telecommunications advise you to look at your overall need to exchange information, by voice and hard copy, now and as you grow. The objective is to determine how a combination of voice, data, and fax services might make you more effective in dealing with your customers, clients, suppliers, and employees. As a limited staff, home-based operation, there is an excellent chance that the skillful use of telecommunications can compensate for that shortcoming and even turn your unique circumstances into a competitive, cost saving advantage rich in the immediately responsive personal service so valued in the marketplace.

Money Management

Telecommunications can bring big time "money management" practices to your home-based business. The term refers to how a business gets the most out of the money that passes through its hands. In brief, the trick to making the most of your business finances involves bringing it in faster, using it as fully as possible (including earning interest) while you have it, and not paying it out any sooner than you have to. Suggestions include such practices as having your customers' credit card payments transmitted immediately to the card company—moving the money from their use to yours more promptly. Collection for problem accounts takes on a personal and immediate tone using telecommunications. Checking on credit as a preventive measure is also a telecommunications supported practice as available to the home-based business as the national supplier.

Telecommunications Ideas to Grow On: Capitalizing on Money Management (1986) offers several recommendations that have applicability to the home-based professional business:

> If you're a consulting type business, let your phone system track long-distance charges and billable time by client for monthly invoicing. If you're selling tangible goods, install a computer system to control inventory and shipping schedules and to capture related financial data. (p. 7)

The same publication goes on to describe the potentially attractive role of banking by computer and using Electronic Funds Transfer in conducting your business' financial affairs. For the limited staff home office practitioner, the following advice is worth noting:

> Banking by computer reduces the work and cost of paper invoices, payroll and bills—while allowing you to control their timing more tightly.

Small companies sometimes find it's more cost-effective to retain a computer bookkeeping service than to start up an in-house operation. (p. 7)

Many efficiencies that are standard operating practices in large firms, may be judged by the home-based business person to be beyond their grasp. AT&T is one of a growing list of providers that would be pleased to show you that this may not be the case. They are aware that 8 out of 10 nonfarm businesses in the United States employ less than 10 people, and they see the potential for making money by showing you how to use their services. Among other things, they will link your home computer to your banking services when you feel your business warrants it (Figure 6–7).

Customer Service

Modern telecommunications services make it possible for you to provide cost-effective direct response to requests for information, complaints, and service requests—just as though you had an established staff dedicated to customer service. There is no way to distinguish between a well-executed response by a home-based businessperson or someone in a traditional operation. The link that you establish with your clients and customers will provide the kind of communication that frees you of paperwork, makes for satisfied customers, and gives you immediate sensitivity to modifications needed to keep your business competitive. The checklist in Figure 6–8 cites situations that lend themselves to telecommunications customer relations solutions. All have applicability in home-based businesses.

Figure 6–7 Electronic banking is a big business convenience available to home-based businesses as well. (Reprinted with permission of AT&T from *Telecommunications Ideas to Grow On* Series. © 1989 AT&T. All Rights Reserved.)

Figure 6–8 A checklist of home-based business requirements that can be satisfied by telephone. (Reprinted with permission of AT&T from *Telecommunications Ideas to Grow On* Series. © 1989 AT&T. All Rights Reserved.)

Telecommunications Ideas to Grow On: Keeping Customers Satisfied (1986) suggests analyzing your calling pattern to select the best supporting services:

- Will most calls occur during or after business hours?
- Are calls clustered during certain times, days, seasons?
- Should you plan more coverage during special promotions or commercial runs?
- Does your market area cross time zones?
- How often might the typical customer call?
- How long will an average conversation last?
- How do you plan to distribute calls when more than one call comes in at a time?
- How do you plan to provide your customer service representatives with the information they will need to handle each call?
- Which particular customer services do you plan to provide—and why?

- Which customer groups are you most interested in reaching?
- What geographic areas?
- How much money are you allocating to your customer service efforts? (p. 8)

Your answers should be framed in the context of your own situation. The home office has to perform some creative adaptation to successfully emulate big business competitors, but the technology is available and effective solutions can be found.

An inexpensive solution is a simple answering machine that takes the callers' names and numbers and indicates a time period when you will return their call. A more sophisticated approach would use a computerized automated response system capable of dealing with most callers directly, taking messages, or directing the caller to a personal response when necessary. Both are discussed more fully under the equipment section of this chapter.

Marketing and Sales

Telemarketing is a two-way electronic street that can carry your services to clients and customers and their responses to you. The scope of your market area is truly unlimited. Figure 6-9 shows you graphically

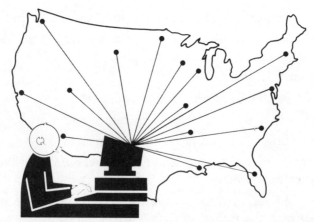

Figure 6-9 A telephone and home computer can connect the home-based business to the nation. (Reprinted with permission of AT&T from Telecommunications Ideas to Grow On Series. © 1989 AT&T. All Rights Reserved.)

what a telephone and a personal computer can do to put a home-based business into the national marketplace.

Telemarketing is an effective way to define and exploit a market niche. Begin close to home and expand regionally, even nationally and internationally, by calling potential clients who have been researched and found to be similar to those you already serve successfully. The more specialized your product or service, the less users per unit of population, so expect to range more widely to identify a viable user group. It can be done using modern demographics and telemarketing—and the home office carries with it no limitations in this regard.

Few home-based businesses can afford the inefficiencies associated with traditional face-to-face selling of your product or service. Figure 6-10 shows where the time of the traditional sales representative is actually spent.

According to AT&T's *Telecommunications Ideas to Grow On: Improving Your Field Sales Productivity* (1986, p. 3) "65% of all sales calls are made to the wrong people, NOT key decision-makers. And, in most businesses, 20% of the accounts generate 80% of the sales! Such statistics show that—if your company operates like most—a little analysis and re-positioned sales effort could produce more profitable results."

A series of hypothetical composites from *Telecommunications Ideas to Grow On: Expanding Your Markets* (1986) illustrate possible uses of telecommunications products and services in home-based businesses. Using some imagination, a modified combination of some of

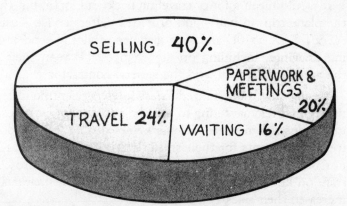

Figure 6-10 The inefficient use of a traditional sales rep's time. (Reprinted with permission of *AT&T* from *Telecommunications Ideas to Grow On* Series. © 1989 AT&T. All Rights Reserved.)

these ideas may trigger a profitable approach from your home office—
perhaps in conjunction with an established business in your area.

- *Opening an International Market.* A distributor of auto replacement parts received occasional calls and letters from military
  personnel stationed overseas who were having difficulty getting
  their American built cars repaired. After doing some telephone
  research, they set up an AT&T International 800 number and
  placed ads in armed forces publications abroad. Supplying crash
  and other after-market items became a profitable adjunct to the
  domestic repair-shop-oriented business.
- *Reaching beyond the Retailers.* A custom T-shirt retailer suffered
  from slack sales at its three mall stores. The owners noted that
  many of its sales were to college-age students, and that some of
  the best sellers spoofed major universities and foreign schools.

  Phone calls to college bookstores produced several orders. On
  campuses where bookstore owners were not interested, they ad-
  vertised in the student newspaper, offering credit sales via an
  AT&T 800 number. Telemarketing more than compensated for
  the decline in over-the-counter sales.
- *Consulting Nationally from the Comfort of Home.* The partners
  in a successful engineering firm in the Pacific Northwest wanted
  to expand their business, but didn't want to leave the lifestyle of
  their small, pleasant city. When they had a chance at a lucrative
  contract halfway across the country, they jumped at it.

  It would mean a lot of traveling back and forth, but they cut
  the plane trips in half—and provided better service—using the
  AT&T FAX 3510D and long distance service to send engineering drawings, including on-site changes, between their office,
  the architectural firm, and the general contractor.
- *Targeting Highly Specialized Sales Calls.* A scientific instrument
  maker uses telemarketing to test the potential of certain specialized industrial markets. Telemarketers qualify leads and schedule appointments for their small, highly technical field force to
  pursue. This strategy allowed the outside salesforce to concentrate on key prospects in these targeted "niche" markets—and
  increased their sales/contact ratio.
- *Computer consulting grows nationally.* Six years ago a two-person
  computer consulting firm started from a Boston office. Astute

market strategy and assertive telemarketing enabled the enterprise to grow into a multimillion dollar business.

Here's how it happened: (1) The partners hired a part-time salesperson to find new business in the Boston area, targeting companies similar to existing clients. He began by making local calls. (2) To explore potential in other Northeast cities, the firm hired a second telemarketer and initiated an AT&T PRO American long distance calling plan. (3) To expand to Midwest and Western markets, a larger telemarketing center was set up, complete with AT&T WATS Service. (4) They opened branches in Chicago and Los Angeles, and called AT&T in to recommend ways to coordinate communications among offices. Meanwhile, all sales efforts continue to be coordinated out of the telemarketing center in Boston.

- *Targeting a Special Food Market Individually.* A line of frozen dinners geared to the nutritional needs and tastes of the elderly enjoyed considerable success in the nursing home market. The manufacturer decided to reposition its product to appeal to a new—and rapidly growing—customer group: affluent senior citizens living at home.

  Now dinners are sold to individuals by telephone—a month's supply at a time—for home delivery. The company supported a telemarketing outbound calling campaign with newspaper advertising and direct mail targeted to retirement communities. A staff dietician conducted free nutrition workshops.

  Customers receive a monthly menu by mail, then use an AT&T CALL ME Card to call in their order, tollfree. If they have not called within a two-day marketing "window," the company places a call to obtain the order.

  Record-keeping, once kept in paper files, is now highly automated. A customer can keep a "standard order" on file, or modify a previous order without repeating the entire thing. Upon request, the company will store an individual's food allergies or special dietary requirements on computer, screening their order against these directives.

  Next year the company plans to expand its area of operations and to establish a regional 800 number.

The specific ideas illustrated should not limit your thinking. Size of the facility or support staff does not rule out a home-based application of similar telecommunications approaches. You can buy outside services —including telemarketing—until you have proven your concept and want to bring it in-house, if ever. These powerful services put your home-based business on a par with larger firms in the creative direct marketing arena, even if you choose to represent products or services obtained externally.

Telephone Company Services

If you live in an area served by computerized telephone switching equipment, there are specialized services available at a nominal monthly charge that will increase the power and versatility of your telephone. It is not necessary to purchase extra equipment; it is all handled by the telephone company's computer that serves your exchange. Here is a list of some options you may find useful for your home office:

- *Call Forwarding* allows you to program your telephone to automatically direct incoming call to any other telephone.
- *Three-Way Calling* lets you have a conversation with people on two other telephone lines—a miniature conference call.
- *Call Waiting* signals you when you are on a call and someone else is trying to reach you.
- *Speed Calling* allows you to program your telephone to dial frequently called numbers by entering a two digit code instead of a the whole telephone number, area code, and so on.
- *Last Number Redial* remembers the last number you called and dials it again when you enter a two-digit code.
- *Cancel Call Waiting* allows you to make a call uninterrupted by the Call Waiting feature, if you prefer—reasons for doing so might include use of a fax or modem, or just not wanting to be bothered during a private call.
- *Saved Number Redial* lets you repeatedly call a number by entering a two-digit code.
- *Busy Number Redial* retries busy numbers and signals you when it has completed the call.

In addition to these options, local telephone companies may provide you with the name and address to go with a given telephone number, or the complete mailing address for a name or number—all for a modest fee. Most will even notify an unlisted number of your desire to reach them. Finally, there are services from banking inquiries to ordering supplies that can be done using your Touch Tone® telephone.

AT&T Alliance® Teleconferencing Service uses your regular telephone to put together a conference call that can include as few as 3 or as many as 58 people located anywhere in the world. It isn't complicated and no operator intervention is necessary. Just dial O + 700 + 456 + 1000 and follow the step-by-step recorded instructions:

- Enter number of locations, including your own.
- Enter each number. In United States: 1 + area code + number. International: 011 + country code + city code + number. When party answers, press # to add them to call.
- Repeat step 2 for remaining telephone numbers. Then add yourself to call by pressing # again.

To end the call, everyone hangs up. It's that simple. (*Telecommunications Ideas to Grow On: Improving Your Field Sales Productivity*, 1986, p. 10) Similar arrangements can be made using the services of other telecommunications vendors serving your market area. You are encouraged to thoroughly investigate the wide range of competitive options available.

CONCLUSION

The home-based professional office would not be very impressive or productive if it didn't have the powerful advantages made possible by the kinds of equipment and services just discussed. It is important to stress that you really *do not* have to be a technical person to become a fully functioning technically literate user of these potent tools. All of the tools were designed (and have been commercially successful) because they are readily usable by *anyone*. Select a level of technology (equipment and software) that is comfortable for you now, then grow through the many levels of sophistication available as you need more. You don't really have a choice—to be a competitive home-based business in the late twentieth century, you can and must have these personal productivity tools by your side.

Chapter 7

Sales-Related Home Businesses

If you are a professional sales representative, you have probably considered the tempting possibility of turning what you are doing now, for someone else, into your own business. The challenge is how to make the transition from a comfortable draw or salary to the irregular commission flow of a freelance marketing person. This is equally true for the salesperson just entering the business. Both need a low overhead base of operations that can sustain them until steady accounts are established and operating reserves are in place.

The home-based business is the ideal place for either approach to a selling career. A residential office can provide all the support needed to pursue traditional outside selling, or to conceive and test far more imaginative, expandable, and technology-backed marketing services.

TECHNOLOGY AND HOME-BASED SELLING

New technologies that opened homes and offices to the sophisticated communications services enjoyed today also turned their occupants into easily identified and approached customers for the purveyors of traditional goods and services. You can market almost anything that is legally sold today nationally from your home to someone else's residence or place of business. The scope and sophistication of your effort is limited only by your imagination and the appeal of your product or service. Being home-based is no constraint.

No More Barriers

Complicated refrigeration is no longer needed to sell Maine lobsters to small town Arizona gourmets or tropical flowers to isolated rural residents, thanks to economical—and fast—delivery services that reach every community. Neither of these products is probably in sufficient demand to be available locally, but a home-based marketing person with drop shipping arrangements from where the products *are* available, can meet the need. If someone is willing to pay for what you offer and you can sell enough to cover your costs and leave an acceptable profit, you can sell *anything* from your home—directly, or increasingly, as a broker for goods shipped from other locations.

Look at the latest AT&T 800 number directory, if you need to be brought up-to-date on what is now being done in direct marketing. There isn't a product or service listed that could not be provided by a home-based business. Whether you could afford the necessary promotional expenses and whether you could generate a profit are other matters to be resolved. Some of the services are anchored in an existing traditional business—many are not. As in any business, you have to figure out how to use the existing opportunities for putting buyers and products together at a profit. This can be done by the home-based businessperson as effectively, if not more so, than their competition facing the overhead of a traditional business.

Does Your Product Stand a Chance?

If the idea of doing this kind of marketing appeals to you, here are some questions needing honest answers as a preliminary test of your product's viability:

- What product—or group of products—do you have in mind?
- Is it or something like it already being sold successfully by direct marketing—the superficial test of "success" is repeated advertising—has the same ad been run for a sustained period?

- Can you compete with the quality and price on the market and still make a profit?
- Can you afford to match competing advertising or find another way to attract sales?
- Can you select a parallel product that would break new ground, but still benefit from the demonstrated success of the established one?
- Is the product available on a private label/drop-shipped basis from a reputable source that will be there to reliably fulfill the orders you will generate?
- Would it be a practical item for you to warehouse personally?
- Can you afford a fair test marketing effort?
- Do you know what a professional presentation of your product would cost—the label, mailing piece, packaging, ad layout, marketing scripts?
- How many sales per thousand calls or mailings would you have to have to make a profit and how does that compare with industry ratios?

Big Time, Small Time, or In Between?

You can check the direct mail literature and begin to determine where you might fit on the scale of possible approaches. The home-based businessperson can start very simply and with both limited resources and objectives. A small ad can be placed nationally for less than a thousand dollars and you can be your own copy writer. The product can be small, nonperishable, and stored in your hall closet. You can add inexpensive telephone supported services to further personalize the process. Small scale doesn't necessarily mean unsophisticated, thanks to technology and services that are now available even for those at the entry level.

Equally possible, depending on your resources and intentions, is a full-scale promotion backed by a complete array of professional services. Identify an advertising agency that has direct mail experience. Ask to see what they have done—you are not interested in funding their education in this expensive field. When you are satisfied that you have a qualified professional capable of delivering what you need, get an estimate for the project. A firm in direct mail advertising can arrange for the necessary services to produce the materials and get them to the buying public through whatever media you select.

You can position yourself anywhere along the continuum from some professional service to none at all. It is possible to start in a limited way relying entirely on your own talents and energy and expand with your incremental success into a wide ranging, highly sophisticated marketing organization—still home-based, but making skillful use of outside mailing services, drop shipping arrangements, and fulfillment houses to handle the mechanical aspects of the business. Your home-office can be the management and the development center for a major enterprise that actually functions, under your direction, outside your home.

A CASE STUDY IN HOME-BASED SELLING

Actual experiences of people who have established sales businesses from their residences best illustrate the pitfalls to avoid and some techniques for converting seemingly terminal problems into successes. The stories that follow are based on actual situations and, together, serve as a general model to examine your own scenario critically. Anticipation of the challenges ahead can make the task easier and more likely to have a happy ending.

Special Regional Products—The Beginning

A young professional couple had recently relocated to the Southeast from another part of the country. Their first Christmas in the area they received a number of gifts that were traditional to the region. Several of the items seemed to have real potential for being marketed in other parts of the country as well.

With no experience whatsoever in direct marketing, they made an approach to the opportunity they saw before them. The first step was to contact the suppliers and see if the products were available to them and at what prices.

Item one was a five-pound tin of local peanuts cooked the old fashioned way. The first marketing question involved whether or not a concept that simple could be conveyed to the rest of the country as anything sufficiently special to warrant ordering at a price considerably higher than the supermarket variety. Informal test marketing with friends convinced them that this would not be a problem—people were easily hooked on the unique product with the common sounding name.

The next consideration was how to store and ship the tins. Here the product's special character began to present problems. While it was not highly perishable, it wasn't something that could sit for more than a few days at room temperature or higher and not begin a process of deterioration.

During peak season from Thanksgiving to Christmas, this didn't pose a major problem. The unheated porch at home was cool enough to hold the product that was ordered in small enough quantities to move rapidly to the customers via a national parcel delivery service. The rest of the year was quite another story. Like most retail businesses, this one did most of its volume in the few months preceding the holidays. What the owners had not really anticipated was that their valued customers would continue to want service—albeit limited—throughout the year.

The problem was solved for the short term with the purchase of a large refrigerator for the storage of the product. It soon became apparent, however, that what was really needed was a freezer. This costly addition could have been anticipated by more experienced marketing professionals. Look for the quirks that might accompany the product or service that you have in mind. They don't need to stop you from proceeding, but addressing them realistically from the outset is more efficient and less apt to lead to unanticipated costs.

Advertising was the next trial-and-error experience. The first lesson is that there is a lead time of several months for the placement of magazine display advertising—and it isn't cheap. Look at the shopping section in the back of your favorite regional or special interest periodical. Next look in the front for the telephone number or address of their display advertising contact. Your request will bring a copy of their rate sheet that tells you the lead time needed, the sizes of space available, discounts for multiple insertions, and such things as the mechanical specifications for your copy.

With the ads designed and placed, the orders actually began to arrive. Along with the ad copy, a local printer had also prepared a combination mailing piece and order form. It all looked very nice and the flow of orders was reasonably steady. A credit card arrangement had been made with the local bank. Chamber of Commerce membership was not difficult to obtain on the basis of good character and professional position in the community. In general, the business was off to a good beginning.

The first holiday season came and went and others followed. A personal mailing list of several thousand regular customers came into being in a card file. It grew larger each year based on continued advertising and an ever widening circle of gift recipients who wanted to share the unique gift with others. A personal computer was acquired to maintain the mailing list and accomplish the necessary correspondence and recordkeeping associated with the business.

Special Regional Products—The Transition

After a few seasons of apparent success and a steadily growing volume of work, our home-based marketing couple decided to take a critical look at what they were achieving. What they saw called for some changes.

Like many people new to the practice of buying, promoting, and selling a product, this couple had developed a lot of smoke but very little fire. The supplier was happy to be moving several thousand more units of product each year, the trucking firm bringing them from the coast to the valley was prospering, the printing company welcomed the challenge, and the customers were happy. How could this be bad?

Profit was lacking. Pricing was being done on an intuitive, instinctive basis that said in effect "What is a fair price for our product?" There was enough good judgment involved to make a modest profit, but all-in-all the margin was not justifying the effort. In order to continue with their operation, the couple needed to do one of two things: (1) Add several dollars to the price of their product or (2) Increase the volume many times over their present rate. Either would give them the profit needed to made their business financially worthwhile. Continuing as they were, the enterprise was becoming too much work for the results being achieved at the bottom line.

When it came to adding several dollars per tin of peanuts, it became obvious that they would be exceeding what the market would bear. There was an additional, related problem. The product was being delivered in the supplier's box and tin. Granted they were inserting their own order forms and literature, but sales were being lost to the name and address appearing on the tin. One solution: Have the supplier package the product in your own tins. Another possibility: Receive the product in bulk and put it in personal tins before shipping.

Both solutions had costs that exceeded the problems they were intended to solve. Designing and ordering small quantities of custom containers is a very inefficient practice—only large production runs result in per unit economies sufficiently large to warrant the effort. On site packaging of a food product became unthinkable from the perspective of health regulations.

The approach that remained was that of greatly increased volume. The only way to achieve it was with a substantial promotional budget for the purchase of mailing lists and the expense of direct mailings. That needed to be accompanied by even larger and more frequent national ads.

They had enough experience by then to know that if their efforts to boost volume substantially succeeded, their storage and shipping facilities would outstrip the capacity of their home. What this called for was an investment that far exceeded the capabilities of this modest home-based business.

Special Regional Products— The Winning Combination

The story just related doesn't necessarily mean that the home-based business failed. For the couple who started it, there was education, growth, and a rational decision not to go on. That determination was one based purely on personal choice and not a limitation inherent in the home setting.

Had it been their goal to develop a substantial marketing enterprise, their product appeared to have the potential to support the effort. It just became apparent that it needed to become something more than what they wanted to commit.

The owners chose to sell their fledgling business to a colleague. She was more interested in growth and found the peanuts to be compatible with a line of country hams that she had sold for several years in much the same manner. In fact, buying the peanut business and expanding both in combination actually solved the same problem for her—promotional costs could be shared and she had a solution in mind for her distribution problems.

Instead of outgrowing her efficient home-based operation, the new owner set about negotiating with the producers of both the peanuts and the country hams. After enlisting the help of an experienced marketing consultant, she concluded that private label drop-shipping was the way to go.

The packaging company that was reluctant to get involved in the project for either small product separately, saw enough potential in the combined venture to make a limited run an acceptable risk. Little profit for the packager now, but the promise of future runs with the start-up costs already behind them. The home-based marketing person had a price she could live with and prospects for savings on future orders.

The happy ending came as everyone involved did what they did best and profited together. As is so often the case, the niche for the home-based sales firm is taking on projects that complement existing businesses by providing them with growth they would not have experienced without the energy and resources of the home office professional. The innovative application of information processing and telecommunications to the national marketing of these two regional products was the proper, and highly profitable, place for this home-based marketing person.

Her ability to focus on taking the products effectively into new markets without the more mundane packaging and shipping chores turned a stalled business into a successful one. As the cost of display advertising increased, so did her ability to extract more orders from each column inch of that costly space. More ad space was devoted to selling the product and less to administrative "where and how to order" by adding an 800-number response system.

When it became apparent that 800 ordering was the way to go and volume reached the point where it was justified, lines were installed to her rural home. Sophisticated telecomputers pleasantly and reliably took orders using a combination of Touch Tone® voice responses 24-hours-a-day, 365-days-a-year. Acknowledgment cards were mailed promptly saying thanks and assuring the customer that the order had been recorded. For the occasional customer who was uncomfortable with the technology, the call was routed via remote call forwarding to the old 800-number order-taking service.

All of this was achieved comfortably in the home office of a beautiful old farmhouse more than a hundred miles from the nearest commercial center or any of the suppliers involved. In time, her proven formula was applied to other products and a major home-based marketing enterprise was perfected and guided toward its owner's objectives.

The product in this case was food. It could just as easily have been an article of clothing or an historic brass reproduction. The secret of success for this home-based marketing operation was a hard nosed look at what combination of price and volume would yield a profit worthy of the effort. Next was the challenge of figuring out how to become a volume marketing organization without giving up the desired focus of the home-based enterprise—an office at home where the owner has the freedom to expand technologically without taking on traditional burdens such as staff and physical plant.

TRADITIONAL SELLING FROM HOME

Selling of almost any kind can have a comfortable base of operations in the home. Technology-oriented national marketing is attractive, but not the only way to go. It is perfectly plausible for you to identify a needed product or service that would normally be promoted from an office or retail site and turn it into a successful home office business.

Brokers and Syndicators

Professional level specialties that involve selling, or "business development," are available for you to exploit in most communities. Those delivering such services are apt to call themselves brokers, syndicators, or something more than a salesman. The approach is to select something that lends itself to up-scale marketing and give it a highly professional image from the home office that portrays the desired status and taste. Insurance is still being sold, but far more professionally—with a strong investment air about it. Syndicated development opportunities are being packaged and sold from the quiet dignity of home offices that impressively accommodate the confidence-building, deal-making nature of that kind of selling. Money brokers arrange for the private financing of business propositions in much the same way. *The Executive Moonlighter* (Wiley, 1989, see Chapter 15) provides an in-depth look at how these enterprises operate.

Telecommunications and personal computer advances have eased the task of the seller "running the numbers" for clients in convincing ways. "What if?" questions are easily addressed using spreadsheet applications so readily available today. Plug in a new interest rate—change the occupancy expectations—alter the cost of some major material—the rest of the pro forma adjusts accordingly.

The presentation continues with a comfortable client whose suggestions are quickly made a part of the model being used to sell him! Conference calls with other principals in the same or distant cities are a simple matter for the home-based professional—so is specialized research or an up-to-the-minute quote on a key stock, interest rate, or airfare. The home office is in no way isolated or limited in its capabilities—unless its owner fails to keep abreast with the fantastic support readily available to him.

Manufacturers' Representatives

In the established selling world, there are manufacturers' representatives ranging the country, territory by territory giving a personal face to a distant warehouse full of products. If you are already a part of this segment of the economy, you have the experience needed to spin off your current product line, or a similar one, and run it from home. You may already be doing that, but with ties that you find too limiting. The answer to achieving the full freedom of how and where to represent your product or service, is as an independent, home-based selling enterprise.

The inexperienced person wanting to enter the field will find it a bit more difficult. He or she may have to start with lesser known lines and build the experience and sales production history required to command the attention of those you ultimately want to represent.

No manufacturer or provider of services is going to want you to be affiliated with an incompatible product line. Other limitations that you might face are things like bonding, to insure that your orders will be fulfilled. Aside from that, you will find that marketing is probably the purest form of capitalism left in our society today. The objectives are totally measurable and when they are achieved, everyone gets what they need to perpetuate the business relationship. The customer receives the wanted product; the manufacturer collects a wholesale profit without venturing into the retail marketplace, and the sales professional is paid well for bringing the two together.

The national trade association for this group is the Manufacturers' Agents National Association (MANA), located in Laguna Hills, California (714-859-4040). They are an excellent source of information on becoming a successful manufacturer's representative.

NEW MARKETING MOUSETRAPS

Terry Moffatt (1989, p. 51) closes his article on the fax machine revolution with a few paragraphs on what is becoming known as "junk fax." If your fax's telephone number becomes known, don't be surprised to find that it is receiving transmissions from people who want to sell you something! Sort of old fashioned cold calling via fax—at night during the most economical transmission hours, of course.

One man's "junk fax" is another's golden opportunity. There is a free market tradition in our country that is not apt to do much in the way of limiting the new commercial routes to your home or office, if they are used with any degree of discretion. The fax is but the latest example of how marketing is using new technology. As a home-based marketing professional, you should take advantage of the efficiencies offered by *legitimate* technological approaches. Unsolicited use of someone's fax machine may not be a good idea—especially in states like Maryland where the legislature just made the practice illegal.

CONCLUSION

The field of sales and marketing always offers lucrative opportunities to new and developing businesses—there is no reason for that to be any less true because you are working from a home office. Refer to the excellent books on the subject of small business marketing in Chapter 15. The home office is also the perfect place to take advantage of the technology-supported selling techniques discussed here and under the telecommunications section of Chapter 6. As a home-based businessperson, you have the flexibility to examine and try a number of products and approaches until you find the right combination for you.

Chapter 8

Providing Professional
Services from Home

Today's home-based professional services range well beyond the
medical and legal practices that were found there for generations.
The kindly general practitioner with the old Victorian house on
Main Street may still exist, and may now enjoy a computer link to
diagnostic centers and teleconferences to keep him abreast of his
field. But the real breakthrough in home-based professional business
is its new viability for dozens of specialists previously bound to traditional settings.

A MATTER OF DEFINITION

If your knowledge and skills are transportable by briefcase and laptop
computer, you may fit the expanded group of new professionals who
are proliferating in the home-based business field. Special task people
who have an in-demand service to sell are increasingly packaging their
businesses as consultants and operating from home offices. The trend
is fed by a combination of affordable home-based technology to support their special functions and a high market value for their services
that is based more on their output than their image.

SOME WHO FIT THE MOLD

Professionals found operating successfully from the contemporary home office include:

Educators

Some have a specialty that lends itself to private practice. What begins as a part-time effort often develops into a full-time home-based business.

College-Bound Counselors

Experts in their field assist college bound students with the competitive application process and the pursuit of financial aid. They find the private dignity of a home office an ideal place from which to conduct the research and dispense the advice purchased by affluent parents impatient with the limited services of the schools. Computers assist in researching college characteristics and requirements, administer and score tests and interest inventories, and prepare polished correspondence to support their applications. Skillfully used technology such as crucially timed teleconferences between admissions officials, students, and parents facilitate the process and add to the air of professionalism.

A Case Study: College-Bound Counseling A woman in the Southwest had been a community college counselor before leaving the field to raise two children. In the process of assisting them with their college applications and pursuit of financial aid, she rekindled an interest in her profession. What she wanted was to do the part of the work that she enjoyed most, leaving aside the bureaucratic hassle of serving on committees, working long nights of mass registrations each semester, and having the freedom to accompany a friend on an interesting trip whenever the opportunity presented itself.

Her approach was to let it be known among the local school officials and her former colleagues that she was available on á consulting basis—from her home office—to assist students with their college applications. She quickly learned that there needs extended beyond making application and her practice grew to include the following services:

- *College selection.* She handled this with popular guidebooks typically available in a school counselor's office and readily purchased at the corner bookstore. What she added was her own familiarity with the references and the institutions that helped students and parents direct their searches more efficiently.

  To this basic service, she added a set of computer disks that contained all of this information and more, plus they are updated more frequently than the published versions. With a personal computer and this software, she was able to efficiently provide a highly professional service that attracted a solid client base.

- *Occupational choice/college major selection.* This was approached by using the standard government and professional references expected in the well-equipped counselor's office. To this she added some interest inventory tests that were available to her due to her status as a trained, experienced professional. What added the extra dimension again was software for her personal computer that let the students take the inventory interactively and see their results immediately. It motivated the students and impressed the parents. More software was acquired that let students use branching logic to narrow down their interests and match them to potential majors and occupations.

- *Financial aid application.* The starting point for financial aid was being certain that clients were aware of government programs. If the parents wanted to provide financial data, she could advise them whether their child would qualify for the various programs, using off-the-shelf financial aid software for her personal computer.

  When she learned that most of her prosperous clients didn't meet the needs tests imposed on government aid recipients, she became a licensee of a firm that specialized in research sources of private financial aid. Using their service, she was often able to identify little known scholarships and grants that were based on the special interests of the donors, rather than financial need.

- *Test taking preparation.* While assisting college bound seniors, she learned that younger members of the same families were preparing for the national level examinations. There was a market for teaching them to be familiar with the style and content of the major exams that mean so much in the college selection process. Again, computer software was available to make the process an effective, interactive tutorial exercise, instead of a routine pencil and paper ritual.

Keeping the home-based business, the counselor could easily hold seminars at an outside location, either to attract potential clients or to deal with larger groups of parents and students at lower rates. The selection of supporting software and reference materials and the degree of individual assistance offered in preparing college and scholarship applications is subject to individual approaches to the practice.

Occupational Choice Counselors

Another specialty that finds application well beyond the student group is that of assisting people in defining their career paths. It can take the form of testing and career exploration supported by special software designed for the purpose.

Specialized Tutoring

There is still a place for the subject matter specialist to assist students who have fallen behind, but the process has grown in sophistication. A home computer with the right software and a qualified teacher can produce results and motivation unheard of in old fashioned tutoring. The stigma is removed and the reward system carefully crafted by experts. In-depth individual treatment is possible for several students in the home-based practice and results can be virtually guaranteed. For qualified specialists, the practice might include working with those who have specific learning disabilities. Computer support accompanied by expert management of the learning process can yield the measurable results for which parents will pay.

Speech Therapy

Speech therapy is an example of a well-defined specialty that lends itself to private practice. Here the practitioner benefits from the privacy of the home office where special equipment supports the therapeutic process. Traditional methods have been augmented by modern computers that do such things as translate speech into visually displayed patterns. The effects of corrective therapy can be instantly visualized by the student and progress recognized by sight. This is another example of genuine professional breakthroughs that are readily adapted to a home-based practice, giving it substance and technical proficiency that add to its commercial viability.

Engineers

Testing laboratories and lofts crammed with draftsmen are no longer the only productive working environments for those who design the nation's buildings, infrastructure, and mechanical and electrical devices. Many of the traditional engineering functions can now be done with computer assistance that allows for endless tests and alterations. For the engineer who is most comfortable as a home-based authority on some aspect of a specialized field, sophisticated desktop computers endowed with the proper software and peripherals provide the power to compete with the best traditional firms. Creative commercial photographer Jook Leung communicates the merger of traditional and computer-based engineering graphics in Figure 8-1 where, for purposes of contrast only, the old fashioned tools are arrayed atop the new, increasingly dominant computerized versions.

A Case Study: Electrical Engineering   A man who had acquired a highly marketable degree from a combination of outstanding universities found himself drawn out of loyalty to his family's small electrical contracting business. After a few years, it became apparent that he was growing stale in his field and passing up some tremendous offers from industry. He joined a major firm, made an impressive salary, worked for a few years, but found himself again unhappy—what he needed was something in between.

This engineer had put together about 10 years worth of experience on both sides of the business—major firm and small contractor. He was constantly being asked for his professional opinion from various sources throughout the industry. He decided to become an independent consultant serving a special role that he had identified, was more than qualified for, and would better enjoy doing.

He felt he could lift a burden from a lot of people in the business by assuming one of their major risks. If he would establish himself as an independent source of expert review for everyone's project plans,

Figure 8–1 The old and new tools of engineering graphics. (© 1989 Jook P. Leung)

they would have a third party shield for a major source of liability. If a component of the contractor's design failed, they could blame him for not catching the flaw in his review.

What this called for was a home-based consulting operation. The clients knew him and were willing to pay for his services. There was no need for a fancy office. The office needed only to accommodate layout tables on which to review schematics and diagrams and a powerful personal computer that could run simulations and other necessary analyses.

The home-based office provided a lifestyle that was particularly attractive to him, and gave him the ability to divert his limited operating capital away from office expenses and concentrate it on the crucial professional liability insurance that would cover his errors and omissions, should they occur. Rates for that kind of coverage were based on his competency and the technical support system that he had amassed to do his job well, far more than the address of his office or design of the receptionist's desk.

This particular engineer created a comfortable and lucrative professional practice somewhere between the family business that couldn't justify his special skills and the huge firm that stifled his independent inclinations.

Computer Specialists

Among the first to capitalize on the work-at-home advantages of their own products were computer specialists. From the legendary software designers who come down from their mountain retreats to bestow another breakthrough application on a waiting user community, to the specialist who works out of an apartment in any major city doing well as a fee-based authority on how to use what someone else invented.

A Case Study: Computer Consultant   A woman with a sophisticated scientific degree grew disenchanted with further graduate study after completing her master's degree. She looked into employment possibilities in her narrow specialty and found them not to her liking. A friend suggested that her penchant for computer programming and systems design might be more marketable than she ever imagined.

Starting out with a few assignments from the friend who got her started, the computer-related consulting business grew. It reached a point where she was sufficiently complimented by a job offer in the field that she took it. What proved to be a good working credential for future freelance consulting assignments, did not turn out to be the kind of work she enjoyed.

With no expensive lifestyle to support, she went back to freelance consulting from her apartment. More jobs led to several on-going accounts. From that base, she was comfortable and found it especially attractive to work with individuals or small team projects.

She gained developer status with computer and software manufacturers and worked on challenging projects that were quite apart from her applications oriented consulting that provided the base for her practice. The urge to add associates and build a larger firm never entered her mind. She enjoyed getting to know the people she worked with and shared in their satisfaction of seeing their businesses grow. Nothing suited her better than to show up at national conferences as an independent—totally free of the corporate limitations she choose not to impose on herself.

This particular computer consultant made an excellent living by performing a limited series of tasks including:

- Conferring with clients on their needs and recommending popularly marketed equipment and software
- Purchasing and installing the equipment and software
- Training the company staff in the use of the systems
- Listening to their requirements change as their sophistication grew and accommodating it with enhancements to their systems
- Modifying the mass market software to meet individual needs
- Performing complex analyses and database projects that proved to be too difficult for the company's personnel
- Independently participating on teams developing new software applications for the industry.

This is an example of a highly generalized computer consulting practice.

It is possible to select a deep technical specialty and establish yourself as a competent practitioner—it is done regularly in expert systems and artificial intelligence. Another direction to take is one based on the knowledge that you acquire in a certain applications software specialty such as word processing or desktop publishing. The expertise you sell is familiarity with the operation of the specialty software, not your ability to do programming or even know much about computers. There is an endless array of special niches that can be defined between the two extremes, depending on the market you feel comfortable serving from your home-based office.

"Generic" Consultants

Name a task that can be done better by applying a relatively obscure expert's skills and you have identified a generic consultant. Narrow, individual specialties that do not stand as identifiable clusters of expertise, fall under this all embracing term. They probably don't have a national association representing them, or they exist as a special interest group within a larger organization.

For the professional who is not bound to his own specialty—perhaps someone who is ready for a change of career or emphasis—the potential of generic consulting may be especially inviting. The bright, experienced person, wise to the ways of an industry can often identify a need and fill it with some adaptation of his own knowledge. He acquires what is needed to make himself a uniquely marketable package— generally in a specialty too narrow to have competing experts emerging from traditional training programs. What's required is an ability to piece together the essential elements of some unique service or solution and then define a broad enough user population to support it.

The home office is an ideal setting for the generic consultant whose expertise is highly marketable in a thin band across a wide selection of users. Whether clients come to him or he travels to their dispersed places of business, it is likely that everything he needs will fit into the conceptual model of a home-based practice.

Syndicators packaging regional deals or diagnosticians applying their own unique models to the problems brought to them for resolution—narrow subject experts whose clients seek the power of their results and not the prestige of the office address. Usually it will be a service not needed frequently enough by a given user to justify gaining the expertise in-house. Often the consultant's unique contribution is an outgrowth of his perspective across an industry, and his professionalism in deftly using that knowledge without compromising the individual clients who contribute it.

There is an unwritten rule of inverse importance ascribed to the simplicity of experts' letterheads and business cards. The generic consultant has arrived when his business card bears nothing more than name, address, and telephone number. His reputation precedes him and needs no embellishment or established firm affiliation. A fitting home office base is the ultimate extension of this understated endorsement.

CONCLUSION

Professional services are always expert in nature. The demand is external and is very directly based on *what* you can do, not *where* you do it. The skills of the professional are highly portable. They are also clean and not disruptive activities. These qualities combine to make such services a natural for the home-based business. The very personalized nature of the expert and his services is often actually enhanced for the client by the home office setting that is so intimately reflective of the person whose services they seek.

Chapter 9

Producing Something at Home

The last two chapters discussed selling things or offering services from home-based businesses. A third possibility for the professional who elects to work from home is *making* a tangible product there. Artists have always thrived in the home studio. Now new technologies are providing the home-based worker with a broader set of capabilities. With these tools, the professional working at home can get beyond the artistically creative stereotypes and generate commercial and industrial products as well.

Things are being made at home today that rival the products of the most sophisticated commercial facilities. The concept of *production* no longer equates to an *assembly line* and being home-based isn't synonymous with limited capabilities. Consider the special areas discussed next.

MUSIC

Michael Jackson and Willie Nelson may not be your typical home-based professionals, but they represent a long line of artists who have brought their production capabilities into their homes. Voices and musical instruments are only starting points for the commercial musical products that command large markets today. Creativity is extended beyond the performing talent of the individual or group to include intricate electronic balance and augmentation. It is achieved with synthesizers and control boards that build a simple performance into a finished commercial production.

Thanks to advances in the same personal computers that make desktop publishing a reality, many of the tricks of the commercial music studios are becoming available to artists who are anything but superstars—yet. Composers, arrangers, and artists can sit at electronic keyboards and watch their performances transformed directly into formal musical notation. Their initial creations can be endlessly augmented and modified with the ease of a machine that can present the standard rhythms, instruments, and so forth, on command.

This is done with a personal computer that has application software oriented toward the creation of a musical score, instead of the spreadsheet analysis of a real estate deal. The keyboard resembles a piano, instead of a typewriter. And the printer churns out cleft notes and staffs, in place of text and numbers. There is a sound generator that will utter whatever is called for by the electronic instructions of the computer. All of it no more amazing than the now ordinary office applications of these desktop wonders, but more dramatic when applied to an art form.

New musical software and supporting hardware will not an artist make, but for those with the talent and inclination, it just might make them *commercially* viable in a competitive, highly commercial business. A home studio can now turn out finished products whose quality will command the respect of those who listen to audition tapes—assuming the creative artistry is there as well.

If you are less of a performing artist, consider the home-based possibilities that the new software products bring to music-related desktop publishing. "Besides generating standard scores and parts, music-notation software has other uses—such as the production of textbooks that use musical examples, songbooks decorated with fancy type and illustrations, music catalogs, and modern scores that combine conventional notation with nonstandard graphics. These projects require functions that lie outside the realm of traditional notation" (Lehrman, 1988, p. 210).

This new specialization has great potential for the home-based professional with the combination of musical and computer skills. This is just one example of how a special niche might be defined to create a commercial music product from a home office with the support of new technology. Figure 9-1 shows how the new music notation software looks on the computer screen.

A Case Study: Producing Printed Music at Home

This home-based businessperson retired from the military service last year. His career was a little unusual—he spent his 25 years on active duty as a professional musician. When this career ended, he was in his early forties. He left with a modest pension and a wealth of experience as a musical technician who spent many years doing the arrangements for prestigious national military bands and vocal groups.

To make a living using the talents he had so successfully cultivated and loved would require staying in a major metropolitan area or teaching in a college. The city option was in conflict with his long-held plans to return to a midwestern farm that had been in the family for generations. First, he contacted several colleges in that rural area and found his services were not exactly in high demand. For one position, he could not be seriously considered unless he completed a doctor's degree in music. Another could offer little encouragement until the incumbent professor retired in about five years.

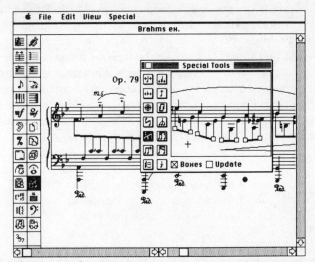

Figure 9-1 Music graphics software as it appears on the screen. (Reprinted by permission from the July, 1988 issue of *Macworld*, published at 501 Second Street, San Francisco, CA 94107)

The solution to his problem came nearly by accident when his son purchased an Apple Macintosh computer and subscribed to several of the user magazines. The father noticed an increasing number of features on musical applications of the Mac. New and more powerful software was rapidly moving it from a novelty to a professional piece of equipment. Figure 9–2 is a summary of the outstanding capabilities currently available in the rapidly evolving field of music graphics software.

One article in particular coincided with his preretirement planning last summer. Christopher Yavelow, himself an accomplished computer-assisted composer, wrote "Music Processing: The Next Generation" in the July, 1988 issue of *Macworld* magazine. Three opening paragraphs of that article described a trend and provided the inspiration for creating a home-based professional who would be in the forefront of a new industry—musical desktop publishing:

> Paul Sadowski, proprietor of Music Publishing Services in New York, is one of this country's finest music engravers. His firm has undertaken major compositions by some of America's foremost composers, including Leonard Bernstein, John Cage, and Gil Evans, and works routinely with such respected publishers as Boosey & Hawkes and C. F. Peters. Sadowski's own engraving has been exhibited at the Philadelphia Museum of Art and the Museum of Modern Art in New York. Noting that "the handwriting is on the wall," Sadowski says Music Publishing has suspended manual operations so that "we can begin getting our hardware and software together. We are going to go with the Macintosh."
>
> Sadowski's feeling that now is the time for computerization is largely a result of the arrival of a new generation of Macintosh music-notation software that promises to do for music publishers, composers, and engravers what PageMaker and company have already done for the purveyors of the printed word. Music publishing is a $500-million-a-year industry in the United States, and the high price of notation preparation—most of which is still carried out by hand—makes it an industry eager for the benefits the Mac can offer. Only a few of the 400 music publishers in this country can now afford to maintain in-house engraving facilities. Nearly all sheet music is currently subcontracted out, with an increasing percentage going "offshore" to Korea, where prices can nevertheless reach six figures for a single symphonic work.
>
> But second-generation notation programs do more than just cut costs via desktop publishing techniques. Developers have combined MIDI capabilities with the best of Macintosh interface design and expert-systems programming to significantly increase the productivity of anyone who wants to notate music. (pp. 102–103)

Short and Suite

Finale 1.7.2

Pros: Excellent for composers, publishers, arrangers, orchestrators, and general musicians. Transcribes complex, rhythmically polyphonic music (including tuplets and meter changes) from MIDI input without a Mac-generated reference click. Retains all performance information. All symbols are MIDI-coherent. Determines guitar chords automatically and outputs user-predefined voicing during playback. Music scrolls by on playback. Configurable to duplicate any engraving style. Built-in MIDI-executable symbol designer. Mirroring option links copies and variations to source. Supports selection of discontiguous regions. Slaves to SYNC.

Cons: Expensive ($1000). Lengthy learning curve for full realization of potential of all available options. Operates best with greater than 1 megabyte of RAM.

HB Music Engraver 1.04

HB Pros: Extensive control of cautionary accidentals. Provides tools for drawing directly on the score. Elegant page-formatting options. Supports gray scale. Midrange price ($395).

Cons: Offers questionable value for a composer or an orchestrator. Most suitable only for simple publication requirements. Clumsy input, very modal. Doesn't follow Macintosh user interface guidelines. Current release not WYSIWYG (though developers claim they are working on it). Developers' attitude: Let customers beta test the software (initial release had numerous fatal bugs).

High Score

Pros: Aimed at general musicians, composers, and arrangers. Optimized to work with Southworth Music Systems' popular sequence programs MIDIPaint and OneStep. Commendable PostScript implementation. Ease of use a primary design concept. Shares files when running under MultiFinder with Southworth Sequencers. Inexpensive ($200).

Cons: Conversion of MIDI data to High Score is a one-way process. No direct MIDI input or output capabilities. First release handles a maximum of 16 staves.

Passport Designs

Pros: Excellent choice for general musicians or copyists. Practical for composers and arrangers. Optimized to work with MasterTracks Pro Sequencer. Interface and features are illustrative of what Professional Composer might have been if Mark of the Unicorn had listened to its users. Will include some film-scoring features: hit lists or tempo maps, can slave to MIDI Time Code. Will include some features aimed at composers. Easy to use. Midrange price.

Cons: No direct real-time MIDI In except through MasterTracks Pro. Limited range of note values: whole note to a 64th note. Questionable implementation of ability to bind lyric syllables to notes.

Music Publisher 1.0

Pros: Excellent for general musician and copyist. Missing some features for composers and arrangers but will fulfill most traditional music publishing requirements. Presto Keyboard provides for extremely fast input. Includes tools for drawing on score, library of tablature, spelling checker for musical terms, and see-through, stick-on key labels for reference. Prints music in columns. WYSIWYG. Closely adheres to Macintosh interface. Easy to learn. Midrange price ($595) includes Presto Keyboard. (Also comes in a professional multiuser version, $895.)

Cons: No MIDI In or MIDI Out as of this writing but developer is rushing to include MIDI implementation. Learning the Presto Keyboard is relatively easy, but getting up to full speed on the alternate Macintosh keycaps may take extra time. Current version allows only singly dotted notes.

Nightingale .70

Pros: Aimed at composers, engravers, publishers, orchestrators, arrangers, and general musicians. Many state-of-the-art features already implemented and more on the agenda. Will include many additional features for composers. Easy to learn. Follows Macintosh interface but adds many innovative power-user features. Supports selection of discontiguous regions. Permits fine-tuning of any symbol's graphic or MIDI parameters. Midrange price.

Cons: Extremely comprehensive and ambitious development spec indicates we may have to wait some time for product release.

Figure 9–2 A sampling of music graphics software. (Reprinted by permission from the July, 1988 issue of *Macworld,* published at 501 Second Street, San Francisco, CA 94107)

With this as his introduction to a yet unborn business, he proceeded to learn all that he could about desktop publishing and the new music software. Last fall, he retired and relocated to the rural midwest. The first few months were spent establishing an efficient home office, taking care of the business necessities of getting organized, and learning the efficient operation of his new music publishing setup.

Since he was breaking new ground, it was productive to go to a nearby university library and do some research. In the business reference area, he was able to locate the names and addresses of potential customers in the music industry, including major publishers for whom he might subcontract as an alternative to their off-shore sources. Publications were identified in which he placed small advertisements inviting readers to send for more information regarding his music publishing service. A list broker was contacted via an advertisement in a national 800 number directory and he was able to purchase the names of several thousand specific firms and individuals who would very likely have an interest in his service—a mailing piece was created on the Macintosh that included a sample of his musical notation work.

By the time six months had passed, our retired military arranger was keeping his family busy responding to inquiries and he was talking with several long time associates who were also about to leave the service to join him in his growing enterprise. The idea was to remain home-based and farm the work out to associates who also worked from their homes—a model he found common in the desktop publishing business. When two of his best prospects bulked at relocating to his rural location, he quickly adapted the system so that they would join him on a temporary basis long enough to learn the operation and then live wherever they pleased. Computer modems, telephone fax, or overnight delivery services would tie them together quite efficiently.

They found that the business was prospering, but there was still a need to stay active professionally. One of them put a notice on the computer bulletin board of the service he subscribed to and was pleased to learn that there was a national user group for music enthusiasts.

This composite example of a unique new technology application for actually producing something from a home office is grounded firmly in fact and reality. The *Macworld* article is real, as is the music publishing trend it describes. This is but one of many powerful capabilities reaching the software shelves each year that create previously nonexistent home-based professional business opportunities. A trip to the library and a few hours of paging through recent back issues of popular computing magazines will almost certainly reveal a breakthrough in a field with which you can identify.

Precision Tooling

There has long been a place for the small machine shop that produces specialized components for larger manufacturers as a subcontractor. Some of these shops are little more than an elaborate home workshop—a home-based business.

Today, precision parts are produced by highly sophisticated computer-controlled machines—not the kind of thing that you would expect to find within the reach of small home-based precision millers. While it would be misleading to say that such operations are a small undertaking that the average person could set up in a garage, home CAD/CAM (Computer-Aided Design/Computer-Aided Manufacturing) operations are becoming a possibility.

Richard Wolfson (1988, pp. 188–196) explains that, "Going from the drawing board to a finished product is the CAM . . . part of CAD/CAM. You just dump what you've designed with a CAD package into a CAM program, and it controls the tooling and milling machines that form the product." He goes on to say that a major machine tool manufacturer's software and supporting products are ". . . bringing CAM within the reach of even small machine shops. Not only is it inexpensive, comparatively speaking, but it also eliminates complex mathematics, so that most machinists are able to run the software. . . . Packages with CNC, tooling, computer, software, and support can cost upwards of $100,000."

Using such a relatively expensive combination of software, desktop computer, and the peripherals needed to link it to production machinery, a home-based shop can turn out components worthy of the space program. The very scope and sophistication of such an operation dramatically defines the difference between what was considered home-based work a few years ago and what can be done there today.

Although, something of this magnitude weighs in at the upper end of the home-based business continuum, it remains a viable possibility for the right person in the right situation. It is now at least possible, thanks to the popularly priced small computers and those who write the software to let them perform production miracles on the cheap. Wolfson (1988, p. 190) concludes that with the new software, " . . . the power to control these machines now resides solidly on the desktop."

If a $100,000 operation is beyond your means, *Macworld* ("Desktop Manufacturing," July, 1988, p. 81) discusses a smaller setup that may be more what the home-based manufacturer would have in mind:

> Computers have replaced the punched tape once used in manufacturing environments to control specially designed machine tools. Now, user friendly Macs are beginning to replace those early, more-difficult-to-use computers. A Macintosh running manufacturing software from Gibbs and Associates can tell a two-foot high milling machine, mounted on your desk, exactly how to manufacture a complicated part.

Still not inexpensive, the full system—including computer, software, and installation—ranges from $9000 to $15,000.

Previously unthinkable home production enterprises are becoming a reality. All that is needed is a programmer to develop the software, an engineer to design the necessary linkages, and the computer's inexpensive and tireless precision that can then manage almost any task.

CAD/CAM production possibilities branch off into directions and levels of complexity that can only be appreciated by those of you who are professionals in the various specialties. The literature of your field and popular computing publications will lead you to a number of interesting home-based production possibilities. If a less obvious solution doesn't materialize, go to the library and find a software company directory (the computer magazines have special issues devoted to such things), identify the companies that sound like they might cater to your interests and call them. If they don't have what you need, ask for the name of some developers and call them—there is a real network among these people and they know what their friends are working on. Find a way to ask that shows your admiration for what they are doing—flattery will still get you anywhere, especially if it is genuine.

Computerized Gourmet Applications

The personal computer has well-known applications in the management of recipe files and shopping lists—early selling points of the home computer. Restaurants now communicate orders from the dining room to the kitchen, monitor their status, control inventory, and generate the tab by the same computer entry.

Gourmet take out has become a big business in major cities where well heeled workers pay for the privilege of having a respectable meal sent to their door. These establishments often begin, and sometimes grow, as home-based businesses. Success and growth are enhanced by available technology in both the telephone and computer areas. For example, fax machines are used to rush dinner specials to restaurant clients before they leave their offices.

Actual home-based production of a gourmet food specialty was recently featured on a local Washington newscast. A woman in suburban Virginia decided that no one in the greater capital area was marketing a respectable Key Lime pie. She had a family recipe and the encouragement of acquaintances who loved her product. The capacity of her residential appliances was soon outstripped by demand. She kept up with the growing business by acquiring a commercial mixing machine. It was microprocessor controlled and provided the necessary volume of high quality Key Lime pie filler, reliably true to her recipe and texture requirements.

This is a modern technology twist on an ages-old home-based business—baking. The difference between the old home produced baked goods business and this application of the latest baking technology business is enormous. With the technological upgrade, a Virginia housewife has been able to hire a few part-time helpers and penetrate a very competitive specialty market in an effective, commercially successful way.

Desktop Publishing

Sometimes a combination of computer equipment and software are so powerful and useful that they create industry revolutions of their own. The Apple Macintosh® computer, its accompanying Laserwriter® printer, and Aldus PageMaker® desktop publishing software did exactly that. Layout of everything from newsletters and advertising flyers to full-length books was moved from complicated composing rooms to cottage industry living rooms.

Apple capitalized on the overwhelming attractiveness of this publishing combination as a device to get their products into otherwise closed markets. Individuals working for government agencies and major companies went so far as to spend their own money to have it available in offices dominated by more traditional desktops that lacked these capabilities.

The ramifications of desktop publishing for the home-based professional remain nothing short of astonishing. Graphic artists, text preparers doing finished work for publishers, and independents totally writing and laying out copy that is ready for the presses all thrive because of desktop publishing capabilities. The new-found economies and total in-house control of the creative process have brought literary products to the marketplace that would have never seen the light of day.

As the process became increasingly popular, so did the proliferation of supporting products to make it even more attractive. Tie the entire process together and you have a chain of home-based professionals linked by a traditional business—the publishing house—that serves as a purchaser for their individual services and distributes the ultimate product. In popular book publishing today it is common for

- A literary agent (working at home) to market the idea of
- A writer (working at home) to
- A publishing house (some of whose editors work at home) to send the manuscript to
- A copy editor who works at home and
- A designer with a home-based office and then to
- A typesetter who uses home-based keystrokers to set the type and send it on to the printer.

The copy is passed along on a computer disk and it all gets developed and refined via the telephone and fax machine.

Similar stories could be related about financial and other special interest newsletters that have been created and maintained through substantial growth by home-based publishers. The traditional practice of having "stringers" or contributors who are experts in their field provide authoritative input from remote corners of the country remains the standard operating mode.

Technology is critical in the deadline sensitive newsletter business where a polished product must get into the hands of subscribers quickly.

- Writers get the latest data for their features by tying in to distant markets and research services via computers and modems.
- They make their input to the publisher's computer either by modem or fax—or a combination of the two that turns the computer into a specialized sort of fax machine.
- It all gets edited and composed without having to be reset because it was received in some computer readable medium—modem communicated code or hard copy is scanned converting it to a digital stream suitable for the computer and its software's "understanding."
- The output may be laser printed as camera ready copy, free of the old dot matrix "computer-look." Another option is digital communication to the print shop's computer driven composer.

The newsletter is ready to be printed, folded, addressed, and mailed using a computer maintained list of subscribers. Even that list becomes another product brokered by others as one more source of income—list rental—to drive the home-based publication business.

CONCLUSION

Production in the home-based business extends to some new and exciting areas, thanks to the computer revolution. The cases discussed touch just the tip of the iceberg. Whether your medium is art, music, or a milling machine, there are possibilities worthy of your attention. The competitive home-based production business of today calls for the precision and efficiency of technology supported tools—and they are available at prices within your reach, now.

Chapter 10

Marketing Yourself as an Independent Contractor

The secret to marketing yourself successfully as a home-based, independent businessperson is to effectively offer a service that others truly need. If you know the rules and establish your business relationships appropriately, you can offer the purchasers of your services much more than your professional talents alone.

There are significant advantages to businesses that can purchase your services and not have you considered an employee. There are taxes they don't have to withhold. There may be liabilities that they can distance themselves from, if not totally escape. In short, the more nearly you portray yourself as a stand-alone entity and not someone who could be construed as an employee, the better the buyer of your services will probably like it.

WHY THEY'RE BETTER OFF NOT "HIRING" YOU

To give you some appreciation of the value of legitimately being an *independent contractor* rather than an *employee,* look at the record-keeping that must be done by employers for each employee. There is no more graphic illustration of why your nonemployee status would be attractive to a company than the IRS's own list of what must be done by an employer for each employee. This list of federal tax record-keeping requirements is taken from the *Tax Guide for Small Business* (1988, pp. 7 and 8).

Records of Employers

You must keep all your records on employment taxes (income tax withholding, social security, and federal unemployment tax) for at least 4 years after the due date of the return or after the date the tax is paid, whichever is later. In addition to the following items required for each specific kind of employment tax, your records should also contain your employer identification number, copies of the returns your have filed, and the dates and amounts of deposits you made.

Income Tax Withholding   The specific records you must keep for income tax withholding are:

1. Each employee's name, address, and social security number

2. The total amount and date of each wage payment and the period of time the payment covers

3. For each wage payment, the amount subject to withholding

4. The amount of withholding tax collected on each payment and the date it was collected

5. If the taxable amount is less than the total payment, the reason why it is less

6. Copies of any statements furnished by employees relating to nonresident alien status, residence in Puerto Rico or the Virgin Islands, or residence or physical presence in a foreign country

7. The fair market value and date of each payment of noncash compensation made to a retail commission salesperson, if no income tax was withheld

8. For accident or health plans, information about the amount of each payment

9. The withholding exemption certificates (Form W-4) filed by each employee

10. Any agreement between you and the employee for the voluntary withholding of additional amounts of tax

11. The dates in each calendar quarter on which any employee worked for you, not in the curse of your trade or business, and the amount paid for that work

12. Copies of statements given to you by employees reporting tips received in their work, unless the information shown on the statements appears in another item on this list

13. Requests by employees to have their withheld tax figured on the basis of their individual cumulative wages

14. The Forms W-5, *Earned Income Credit Advance Payment Certificate*, of employees who are eligible for the earned income credit and who wish to receive their payment in advance rather than when they file their income tax returns.

Social Security Taxes   You must also maintain the following information in your records on the social security (FICA) taxes of your employees:

1. The amount of each wage payment subject to FICA tax

2. The amount of FICA tax collected for each payment and the date collected

3. If the total wage payment and the taxable amount differ, the reason why they do.

Federal Unemployment Tax Act   The Federal Unemployment Tax Act (FUTA) requires you to maintain the following information in your records:

1. The total amount paid to your employees during the calendar year

2. The amount of compensation subject to the unemployment tax

3. The amount you paid into the state unemployment fund

4. Any other information required to be shown on Form 940, *Employer's Annual Federal Unemployment (FUTA) Tax Return*.

Federal tax recordkeeping is only one reason why a potential user might find an independent person's services more attractive. Others include the trouble and expense avoided by not including you in employee benefits such as insurance and pension plans. You carry your own liability insurance and are not a part of the organization.

Defining the Independent Contractor

As an independent contractor, you take on the burdens of a fully self-employed person with all the obligations of tax withholding and those things normally associated with an independently functioning professional in your field. The *Lexicon of Tax Terminology* (Westin, 1984, p. 352) gives the following definition:

> **Independent contractor:** an individual subject to the control and direction of another only as to the result of his or her work, and not as to the means. . . . The term independent contractor is complementary to the term employee in that they each represent different employment relationships but together they include all employment relationships. However, since the term employee is broader in scope for purposes of Social Security tax (FICA) and federal unemployment tax (FUTA) than it is for purposes of income tax withholding, the term independent contractor is correspondingly narrower in scope for purposes of FICA and FUTA than it is for purposes of income tax withholding.

Since there are tax and even social justice ramifications, a body of law and administrative tests has developed around the independent contractor concept. Familiarity with these items will help you understand what must be done to represent yourself correctly and appreciate the difference between your situation and that of those who may see it as a threat to fair compensation and benefits.

Legal Points   Kathleen Christensen (1987, p. 20), Director of National Project on Home-Based Work, City University of New York Graduate Center, a group studying the impact of telecommuting on women, offers the following guidance from California law on defining the independent contractor:

> . . . the question of whether a worker is an employee or an independent contractor generally revolves around the following questions:
>
> • How much control does the worker have over the execution of the work?
>
> • What is the worker's opportunity for profit or loss?

- Has the worker made a large investment in the enterprise? Does he or she have a place of business and offer services to the public?
- What is the worker's level of skill?
- How permanent is the relationship?

Generally, an independent contractor exercises control over the execution and timing of the work, has the opportunity to gain or lose, has made an investment in equipment or capital, has a skill that allows him or her to compete in the marketplace, and is not in an enduring relationship with the employer.

The corollary holds true: If the worker has little control over work hours, priority, or pacing of the work, has no opportunity to gain or lose, uses materials, tools, or equipment from the employer, and has an ongoing relationship with the company, then he or she is entitled to the rights and protection accorded by law to company employees.

Practical Actions   Steven Tomczak is an authority on professional consulting in the technical fields. He lists what it takes to make yourself a free-standing practitioner in the eyes of companies for whom you may find yourself working. These are some of the tangible proofs of having established yourself as a legitimately independent professional whose claim to contractor status will likely be defensible:

- A business license obtained from your city clerk
- Articles of Incorporation, if you are incorporated, from the Secretary of State where it is registered
- A fictitious name statement filed with the appropriate agency, if you are unincorporated and not operating under your name
- A Certificate of Insurance proving Worker's Compensation coverage
- A Certificate of Insurance showing your liability coverage
- An Employee Identification Number from the IRS

(Adapted from Tomczak, 1982, p. 65)

In the Eyes of the IRS   From the point of view of the federal tax authorities, everyone is an employee who does not make a compelling argument for being otherwise. An established business organization can be relied upon to report on the activities of its employees and withhold the appropriate taxes. In the Carter Administration, for example, legislation favorable to independent contractors was discouraged with claims that ". . . 50 percent of all independent contractors were failing to comply with payroll tax and federal income withholding requirements. The resulting revenue loss—estimated at that time to be in the neighborhood of $6 billion per year. . . . " ("The Agent, His Independent Contractor Status and the IRS, 1983, p. 3). Here is what the IRS has to say on the subject from *Tax Guide for Small Business* (1988, p. 118):

Who Are Employees?

Before you can know how to treat payments you make for services rendered to you, you must first know the business relationship that exists between you and the person performing those services. The person performing the services may be:

- An independent contractor
- A common-law employee
- A statutory employee
- A statutory nonemployee

Independent Contractors. People such as lawyers, contractors, subcontractors, public stenographers, auctioneers, and so on, who follow an independent trade, business, or profession in which they offer their services to the general public, are generally not employees. However, whether such people are employees or independent contractors depends on the facts in each case. The general rule of thumb is that an individual is an independent contractor if you, the employer, have the right to control or direct only the result of the work and not the means and methods of accomplishing that result.

You do not have to withhold or pay taxes on payments you make to independent contractors.

Common-law employees. Under common law rules, every individual who performs services that are subject to the will and control of an employer, as to both *what* must be done and *how* it must be done, is an employee. It does not matter that the employer allows the employee discretion and freedom of action, so long as the employer has the *legal right* to control both the method and the result of the services.

Two of the usual characteristics of an employer-employee relationship are that the employer has the right to discharge the employee and the employer supplies tools and a place to work.

If you have an employer-employee relationship, it makes no difference how it is described. It does not matter if the employee is called an employee, or a partner, co-adventurer, agent, or independent contractor.

It does not matter how the payments are measured, how they are made, or what they are called. Nor does it matter whether the individual is employed full time or part time.

No distinction is made between classes of employees. Superintendents, managers, and other supervisory personnel are all employees. Generally, an officer of a corporation is an employee, but a director is not. However, an officer who does not perform any services, or performs only minor services, and who neither receives nor is entitled to receive any pay is not considered to be an employee.

You may have to withhold and pay taxes on wages you pay to common-law employees.

Statutory employees and statutory nonemployees are classes of workers created to deal with the unique situations of certain kinds of salespeople and some individuals who perform very specific work at home for a controlling employer. The purpose is to treat them differently for income tax, social security, and federal unemployment tax purposes.

"The Agent, His Independent Contractor Status and the IRS" (1983, p. 3) quotes the 20 points contained in Internal Revenue Service Training Manuals 8463 and 3142-01 used to determine whether a person is an employer or a contractor. The discussion ends with the following conclusions:

> It's apparent that the IRS guidelines for independent contractor determination, while paralleling the broader, theoretical tone of the legal doctrines, are significantly more detailed and seek to get at the mechanics of an independent contractor-principal relationship. Of particular importance to agents and manufacturers are the questions regarding oral or written report requirements, whether the independent contractor can work for a number of firms at the same time, reimbursement of expenses and continuity of the relationship. Also significant here is [the] question . . . dealing . . . with termination without reprisal. Most agency agreements are written so that either party may terminate a relationship with 30-, 60-, or 90-days' notice. This in and of itself is indicative of a business-to-business, independent contractor-principal relationship, not one of employer-employee.
>
> But the one constant in both descriptions of independent contractor status—the one on which all other deciding factors are based—is the element of control. This is the first thing that will be examined if an independent contractor relationship is questioned for any reason, whether a question of law or a tax dispute. Following that will be the other criteria: whether reporting requirements are present—they, too, indicate an element of control; whether expenses are

reimbursed—implicit here is control over the manner in which a job is done; whether the "tools" to perform a task are provided. No one factor proves or disproves the existence or nonexistence of an independent contractor/principal arrangement. Rather, all in combination with the circumstances surrounding any one independent contractor relationship will determine just where a manufacturers' agent stands with his principals, or where a principal stands with his agents.

While this particular examination of the law and regulations is from the perspective of manufacturers' agents and the firms they represent, the conclusions are applicable to anyone attempting to represent himself or herself as an independent contractor. Similar tests are applied when the question is one of legal rather than tax liability, such as injuries done by an agent operating an automobile in the course of business activities. The body of law used to address these issues is known as "agency law."

Combine the legal tests quoted from Dr. Christensen's article and the tangible proofs of establishing a business adapted from Dr. Tomczak's book and you have an effective checklist for determining how you measure up as an independent contractor. Add to that a layman's appreciation for what the IRS is looking for from their perspective of making a person an employee unless proven otherwise, and you have what you need to know to position yourself successfully as an independent contractor.

THE EXPLOITATION ISSUE

As you operate as an independent contractor on the professional level, you should understand that the concept is considered controversial in other quarters. While independent contractor status may give you the freedom to do exactly what you choose in marketing your services at a substantial fee, some employers have been accused of using the device as a means of forcing employees off payroll and benefits.

Dr. Christensen's comments used earlier to help define independent contractor status were made in the context of a Conference Board article ("A Hard Day's Work in the Electronic Cottage," 1987) that is at times critical of how independent contractor status can be exploited by employers to unfairly deny benefits and fair pay. She cited examples on both sides of the dispute. One of the negative situations involved an insurance company that encouraged a group of claims processors to become contractors and work from home with no salary or benefits. The freedom from the office and commuting was attractive to them, but they ended up feeling that they had been taken advantage of. On the positive side, a major telephone company and a national mail-order retailer were cited as examples of how the work-at-home concept can work well. In both cases, the home-based workers remained in an employee status, rather than that of an independent contractor.

This book is addressed primarily to people who have the skills necessary to command substantial fees for their services and prefer to do so independently. In such an environment, the independent contractor status can be a highly desirable one that can meet important needs of both the offerer and the purchaser of professional services. For an increasing number of salaried professionals, the grass can be greener on the other side of the fence where they are free to command the highest fees available, working as hard as they choose to.

Careful attention should be paid to the points made by Dr. Christensen, however. You should also be prudent about evaluating your potential in the marketplace before you forego the salary and benefits of your present position. If you have any misgivings, consider the possibility of proving the viability of your independent contractor status on a part-time basis.

APPLYING THE INDEPENDENT CONTRACTOR CONCEPT

There are two sides of the independent contractor coin that may be of interest to the home-based businessperson. In the first instance, you are using it as a means to promote yourself—no employer paperwork or benefits expenses for the firm hiring you. A less obvious application is when *you* become the person in need of services and hire someone as an independent contractor to perform a necessary service or as a subcontractor on a project that you are running.

Here is a clause that Steven Tomczak inserts in his contracts with subcontractors in an attempt to make their status clear. Read it in two contexts. First, as he intends it, as a statement to clarify that you have someone working for you who is an independent contractor responsible for their own work, taxes, and benefits. Next, note how the same statements could be modified to convey your own independent contractor status to a potential client. What follows will show you an applied version of how the general concept can be employed:

> *Independent Contractor Status.* The services to be rendered for and on behalf of STEVEN P. TOMCZAK AND ASSOCIATES to Client shall be subject to the control of STEVEN P. TOMCZAK AND ASSOCIATES merely to the extent of the result to be accomplished by the work and not as to the means and methods for accomplishing the result.
>
> In performing services under this Agreement, Consultant shall operate as and have the status of an independent contractor and shall not act as or be an agent or employee of STEVEN P. TOMCZAK AND ASSOCIATES.
>
> Consultant's activities will be at his own risk and Consultant shall not be entitled to Workmen's Compensation or similar benefits or other insurance protection provided by STEVEN P. TOMCZAK AND ASSOCIATES; on the contrary, Consultant will make his own arrangements for payment of hospital and medical costs in connection with any injury or illness and other insurance coverages for the activities to be performed hereunder (Tomczak, pp. 295–296).

Neither Dr. Tomczak nor I am in the business of rendering legal opinions and you should seek the advice of your attorney before attempting to word any contract.

WHAT ABOUT CONTRACTS?

You should always provide your services under the terms of some sort of written agreement. This can be a useful means of defining your independent contractor status. The other advantages of having the terms in writing include the lessened chance for misunderstandings on the product to be delivered, the time for completing the work, and the compensation—including reimbursement for project-related expenses.

In some cases, a simple letter of agreement is adequate. In others, you should negotiate a formal contract. A common practice is to make the proposal a dual purpose instrument that can become the contract, if the terms are acceptable and if it is signed by both parties. Many professional associations have developed model contracts for people doing business in their particular specialties. If you are engaged in such a practice, contact your professional groups, secure sample contracts, and let your attorney benefit by their years of experience in the specialty. One such organization that has extensive offerings in the contracting area is the National Society of Professional Engineers, 2029 K Street, NW Washington, DC 20006. The same is true of most professional groups where it is common for their members to enter into contracts for their services.

Methods of Payment

When your contracts are prepared in your independent contractor capacity, one of the key considerations is the method of payment. The following terms are generally self-descriptive and represent the commonly used options:

cost plus fixed fee	lump sum
cost-plus	payroll costs plus a factor
direct labor cost plus a factor	per diem
fixed fee	percentage
hourly rate	unit price

This list was adapted from Tomczak's Chapter 8, Determining and Structuring Your Fees (1982, pp. 87–102). His book is an excellent resource for this topic.

Topics for the Contract

Tomczak's book also contains 100 pages of sample professional contracts representing a rich variety of possible situations (pp. 233–333). A review of those sample contracts suggest the following list of topics to consider including in your contracts:

arbitration to settle disagreements	cost anticipated
compensation arrangement	definitions of terms
controls to be implemented	general conditions
copyrights, patents, etc.	independent contractor status

insurance provided	reimbursable expenses
introduction	reports to be produced
nature of services provided	schedule of work
objectives of the project	security for projects
payment method	termination arrangements
records to be maintained	time for completion

These topics are listed to illustrate the potential complexity of the arrangements into which you may enter as an independent contractor. The assistance of a competent legal adviser is essential in contracting, but this list may be helpful in your discussion of just what might be necessary in your particular circumstances.

Cost Breakdown

A third contracting concept that Tomczak (pp. 100–101) views as essential for the independent contractor is the proper expression of your costs, when requested. Many times, simply billing your client for the number of hours, days, or a fixed fee is acceptable—other times it is necessary to spell out the differences between your direct and overhead expenses. Refer to his book or a similar reference for a more detailed discussion of costing your projects, but be aware of these basic considerations. Your costs usually will fall into one of these categories:

1. *Direct costs, payroll.* All of your project-related salary and wages presented as hourly rates (annual salary less benefits divided by 2080)

2. *Direct costs, non-payroll.* All project related nonsalary expenses for special equipment, consultants fees, telephone and other communications costs, computer services, travel and expenses, legal fees, laboratory charges, printing, and and so on.

3. *Indirect costs.* Combined indirect costs equal overhead—payroll connected taxes and benefits; general and administrative expenses such as office costs, insurance, professional fees, depreciation, advertising, motor vehicle operation and maintenance, and all of the nonpayroll background costs associated with running your business.

PROMOTING YOURSELF AS AN INDEPENDENT CONTRACTOR

The innate attractiveness of the independent contractor's potential for limited tax and legal liability is a plus in trying to attract business, but it alone will not assure your success. Marketing still means finding opportunities to showcase your talents and services.

The traditional methods of having a well-prepared professional resume, cover letter, and supporting information sheet are essential to finding customers for what you do. Target your resume and information sheet so that the emphasis is on the qualifications and performance factors that really mean something to those in a position to buy your services. Spare them the expanded version that probes the depths of your character, family, and community service accomplishments—save those for nice human touches at the point of personal contact, for those who indicate an appreciation for such things.

Take a businesslike attitude toward every professional meeting, conference, and working group whose audiences contain people in a position to pay you substantial fees and vouch for your competency. Do not be modest. Get yourself on the program of conferences that can be of benefit to you. Write articles and letters reacting to other peoples articles—in a word, make yourself known among those who can help you.

Meeting planners, whether for national conferences or small regional professional meetings, are usually anxious to hear from anyone willing to make a presentation—doubly so, if the topic and the qualifications of the presenter are first rate. Teach a course at a local college. Speak to civic groups. Any and all of these activities can lead to a demand for your services as an independent contractor.

A FINAL CHECKLIST

As you set about establishing yourself as an independent contractor, here is author-attorney Robert L. Davidson's suggested list of do's and don'ts. This list was adapted from a draft of his forthcoming practical and authoritative book on the entire independent contractor concept, to be published by John Wiley & Sons, New York.

- Do try to be paid by the job, not open-ended by the hour.
- Don't become an extension of regular company business.
- Do, within reason, set your own work hours.
- Don't become a full-time, continuing pseudo-employee.
- Do have your own company headquarters.
- Don't be prevented from contracting with others.
- Do have written contracts for your jobs.
- Don't, where possible, use the customer's tools.
- Do make public solicitations for other customers.
- Don't accept fringe benefits from customers.
- Do keep accurate financial records.
- Don't accept employee-like favors from customers.
- Do hire your own staff to work on your contracts.
- Don't let the customer hire your assistants.
- Do avoid responding to "help-wanted" ads.
- Don't set a regular pattern of daily or weekly hours.
- Do have business cards, circular or brochure, invoice forms.
- Don't use any identification symbols of the customer.
- Do have your own liability insurance.
- Don't accept out-of-contract expense reimbursements.
- Do have your own professional licenses and business permits.
- Don't make regular use of customer's office space.
- Do stay separated, where possible, from customer employees.
- Don't attend customer staff meetings.
- Do maintain your own detailed cost-accounting records.
- Don't agree to accept detailed employee-like job directions.
- Do define the scope of the work clearly in writing.

Use this checklist to analyze your particular situation, then review this chapter. As is so often the case, doing things the right way may be no more difficult than doing them the wrong way. Knowing what the acceptable answers should be and arranging your activities to demonstrate that you comply, can be the key to having a happy ending should you be audited in this highly interpretative area of the tax law.

In order to protect vital personal interests, you need to appreciate the ramifications of the independent contractor concept as it applies to the home-based worker. This is equally true if you work at home as a company employee or as a free-wheeling entrepreneur. It is the device used to classify you for tax purposes and it establishes your legal relationship with employers or clients. All of this can have an important impact on how you operate your home-based business and your rights to valuable benefits—whether acquired as an entitled employee, or provided under tax favored aspects of regulations for the self-employed.

Chapter 11

Getting Organized: Legally and Personally

Organizing your home-based business has two dimensions and both warrant early attention. The first is your *legal* form of organization—sole proprietorship, partnership, or corporation—your choice will affect how you conduct the formal side of your business—taxation, liability, contracting, and so on. Second is your *personal* approach to managing the home office and the business activities emanating from it. Self-management is the big consideration here—while it can assume an informal air in the home-based enterprise, you won't succeed without doing it effectively.

LEGAL FORMS OF ORGANIZATION

The starting point of your formal obligations as a home-based businessperson is selecting the appropriate legal form of organization. Here is a preliminary overview of the three choices:

- *Sole proprietorship,* in which *you literally are your business,* share its obligations and rewards with no one, and stand unquestionably liable for its debts and commitments.
- *Partnership,* where the risks and rewards are shared with at least one other person with whom you have agreed, not necessarily

151

in writing, to conduct business for the purpose of making a profit. Unless otherwise limited by the partnership agreement or statute, you and your partner will share the effort, profit, and liabilities equally. For most purposes, the partnership is *not* a legal entity that acts independently of the individuals who comprise it—*you and your partners are your business.* There is no continued life for the partnership after the death of a partner, unless stipulated in the agreement.

• *Incorporation,* where your business becomes a legal entity created by the state with powers, obligations, and a life of its own. It is a formal organization whose formation and operation must respect strict procedures defined by your state. Stockholders elect directors and vote on changes to the articles that formed the corporation. They share in its liability only to the extent of their investment in it and their stock can generally be transferred without approval. *The corporate entity is your business;* it can sue and be sued and generally acts as does the more personal, human sole proprietor or partner in the simpler forms of business organization.

A more detailed discussion of these legal organizational options follows. Although not exhaustive, this discussion offers you an appreciation for what is to be gained and lost by choosing the various options. You will also discover why the choice may not be as simple as you think.

Sorting the Organizational Options

Your choice should be made after full consideration of all three business forms. Arnold S. Goldstein is a senior partner in a Boston law firm and he specializes in corporate law. In his book *Starting Your Subchapter "S" Corporation: How to Build A Business the Right Way,* he makes a series of important points to guide those facing the legal organizational choice. These checklists were adapted from his book with permission.

Important Factors to Consider

• Liability and personal exposure
• Costs including filing fees
• Management structure and whether it needs to be centralized or dispersed

- The available methods of raising capital
- The ability to attract and keep key personnel through various fringe benefits or participations such as stock options
- Tax considerations.

The checklists that follow give you the information needed to apply Goldstein's criteria to your situation.

Specific Advantages and Disadvantages In helping you make a decision on what type of organization is best for you, Goldstein spells out the pros and cons of the three fundamental forms of business organization:

Sole Proprietorships

+ Low start up costs since legal and filing fees are at a minimum. However, many states and cities require at least a filing with the county clerk especially if a fictitious business name is adopted.
+ Greatest freedom from regulation
+ Owner is in direct control.
+ Minimum working capital requirements
+ Tax advantages to owner of small businesses
+ All profits inure to the owner.
− Unlimited liability. The proprietor is responsible for the full amount of business debts no matter how incurred, which means that his personal property may be taken to cover debts of the business.
− Unstable business life, since the sole owner's death or illness would terminate the business
− Difficulty in raising capital and in obtaining long-term financing. (p. 2)

Partnerships

+ Ease of formation (although more complicated than the sole proprietorship)
+ Low start-up costs, especially since there usually are fewer filing fees and franchise taxes

+ Limited outside regulation, unless the type of business itself is one that is in a regulated industry

+ Broader management base than a sole proprietorship and a more flexible management structure than the corporation

+ Possible tax advantages, since it avoids the double taxation of corporations, and because income can be taxed at personal income rates. Naturally, the personal income situations of the partners could also make this a disadvantage.

+ Additional sources of capital, and leverage by adding limited and special partners

+ Each partner can bind all the co-partners, and, in the absence of restrictions in the partnership agreement, may terminate the partnership.

+ The duration of the entity can be limited to a stated time, or can continue indefinitely by amendment.

– Unlimited liability of at least one partner and except in limited partnership situations all the partners have unlimited liability. The personal assets of each of the general partners are available to satisfy partnership debts.

– Life of a partnership unstable since changing partners by adding new ones or by death or departure of partners causes the partnership to terminate.

– Obtaining large sums of capital relatively difficult as the financing cannot be obtained from the public through a stock offering

– Acts of just one partner, even unauthorized acts in many cases, bind all the partners.

– Individual partnership interest cannot be easily sold or disposed of.

– Most tax-supported fringe benefits like pension and profit sharing arrangements available only to corporations are unavailable to partnerships. (pp. 3 and 4)

Corporations

+ Limited liability, that is the owners are liable for debts and obligations of the corporation only to the extent of their investment in the corporation, with the exception that they can be personally liable for certain types of taxes such as payroll taxes which have been withheld from the employees pay checks but not paid over to the IRS and state sales taxes. If the business fails or loses a lawsuit the general creditors cannot attach the owners homes, cars and other personal property.

+ Capital raised more easily than in other forms of ownership. This does not mean, however, that a new corporation can easily sell stock. In the first place, the sale of stock is highly regulated by both federal and state governments and obtaining bank loans for a fledgling business may be no easier for a new corporation than for a partnership or proprietorship.

+ Ownership more easily transferable including transferring shares to family members as gifts or otherwise as well as selling your interest to some other person; however, in many small corporations it is advisable to put restrictions on transfer of shares especially if the persons owning and working in the business must be able to work closely together. This is generally done in the form of a stockholders' agreement.

+ Since the corporation is an independent legal entity, it has a life of its own or continuous existence. It does not cease just because one of the owners dies or wishes to retire.

+ Centralized management which usually rests in the board of directors and is exercised by the officers

+ As a legal entity, it can enter into contracts and sue and be sued and the consent and signature of the owner is not necessary.

+ Has built-in impetus to increase the capital by reinvesting it, since salaries are normally set at the beginning of the year. In addition, surplus earnings can be set aside for a future date, although there are Federal tax penalties if these surpluses exceed certain amounts.

+ Receives corporate discounts, indicating a preference for corporate accounts

+ Retirement funds such a Keogh, defined-contribution plans, money-purchase plans, and other profit-sharing, pension, and stock option plans offer greater benefits to corporations.

− Subject to more governmental regulations than partnerships and sole proprietorships

− May be a more expensive and complex form of business to organize

- Recordkeeping requirements can be very extensive.
- Operating across state lines can be complicated because of the need for corporations to "qualify to do business" in states where they are not incorporated.
- Ending the corporate existence, and in many cases even changing some of the structure if it requires an amendment to the certificate of incorporation, can be more complicated and costly than for partnerships and proprietorships. (pp. 4 and 5)

Additionally, the corporation is a person for tax purposes. That can result in taxation as both corporate profit and again as dividends received by the shareholders. Conversely, corporate losses are not transferred to the shareholders as a deduction. These things are true of the traditional C Corporation—they are the reason for the creation of the S Corporation that gives many of the advantages of traditional incorporation while retaining some of the favorable tax positions of proprietorships and partnerships.

The S Corporation Option

Tax Guide for Small Business (1988, p. 108) sums up the essence of the S corporation in the following two sentences, "Some corporations may elect not to be subject to the income tax. If a corporation qualifies, its income usually will be taxed to the shareholders. These corporations, formerly known as Subchapter S corporations, are called S corporations." The relative attractiveness of S corporation status for the owner of a home-based business usually depends on the following points and how they impact your particular tax and business situation:

- *Avoid double taxation.* Regular corporation income is taxed to the corporation and again to the individual as dividend income. Normally, S corporation income is taxed only to the individual shareholders.
- *Deduct corporate losses personally.* Losses of a regular corporation remain within the tax structure of that corporation; an S corporation loss can be taken personally by shareholders.
- *Lower maximum tax rates.* S corporation income passed through to individual shareholders is subject to personal tax rates that

currently top out at 28 percent versus the higher top corporate rate of 34 percent applied to regular corporations.

- No *double taxation on the sale of assets*. The gain from the sale of assets passes directly to the shareholders of the S corporation, escaping the dual taxation experience within the regular corporate organization.

S corporation may be better if you:

- Don't need to raise a lot of capital since it has a limited number of stockholders, classes of stock, and is generally more restricted in terms of who can participate—contribute capital
- Expect to have property appreciate rapidly, since the gain would only be taxed once
- Expect start-up losses to pass through to individual shareholders.

C Corporation may be better:

- Until income exceeds $75,000 (corp rates are 15 percent first $25,000; 25 percent for the next $50,000; then 34 percent for income over $75,000—at that point the 28 percent personal/S corporation rate may be more attractive
- If you want to accumulate earnings in order to diversify. (S corporation is taxed even if the earnings are not distributed; the C corporation is not.)

Comparing Your Organizational Options

One factor in your choice of organization may be the extent to which it permits you to provide tax-favored fringe benefits to you and your employees. Figure 11-1 is a summary of what the options are under the main categories.

Exploding a Corporate Myth

One of the popular reasons for incorporating is the "corporate shield" that it protects you from personal liability—to limit your losses to your

AVAILABILITY OF FRINGE BENEFIT

FRINGE BENEFIT	C CORP. EMPLOYEE	2% S CORP SHAREHOLDER	EARNED INCOME PARTNER	PASSIVE PARTNER	SELF-EMPLOYED
Health & Accident	Yes	No	No	No Yes under new law to 25%	No
Group-Term Life	Yes	No	No	No	No
Qualified Group Legal	Yes	Yes	Yes	No	Yes
Education Assist.	Yes	Yes	Yes	No	Yes
Dependent Care Assistance	Yes	Yes	Yes	No	Yes
No-Additional-Cost Services	Yes	Yes	Yes	No	No
Qualified Employee Discounts	Yes	Yes	Yes	No	No
Working Condition Fringes	Yes	Yes	Yes	No	No
Diminimus Fringe Benefits	Yes	Yes	Yes	No	No

Figure 11–1 Fringe benefits available to individuals under different kinds of business organizations. (Reprinted from *Starting Your "S" Corporation,* by Arnold S. Goldstein, © 1988, John Wiley & Sons)

stockholder investment in the corporation. It is important to remember, however, that this "shield" has some large holes in it and they are particularly applicable to the small home-based business.

The *alter ego doctrine* is a legal phenomenon used by the courts to reach beyond the corporation and deal with the responsible individuals who comprise it, if an injustice is to be remedied. Simply because you have filed the necessary papers to form a corporation in your state does not mean that you are no longer touchable, should your business incur debt or otherwise wrong someone.

Obvious reasons for a judge to "pierce the corporate veil" and impose personal liability include such things as using the organization for fraudulent or criminal purposes. But the concept goes on to embrace things that you might more easily find yourself accused of—like using your corporation to promote what is determined to be a wrongful purpose or to commit an injustice. There is room for a lot of interpretation that could quite possibly snare you as a home-based business. Corporate bankruptcy to avoid the payment of debts is routinely attacked by an attempt to invalidate the corporation.

According to Hoeber (1980, pp. 824–825), the most frequent application of the *alter ego doctrine* is to one-person corporations and it is commonly used against "close-corporations." What the court looks for includes a list of problems often associated with the home-based small business start up:

- Undercapitalization
- Commingling of personal and corporate business
- Failure to hold board meetings
- Inadequate corporate minutes

The factors involved vary by state. But incorporation, while a tremendously valuable form of small business organization that has many advantages, including the liability limitations, is itself always limited by the good faith of its principals.

You can form a corporation following the steps laid out in the do-it-yourself incorporation kits. Whether you end up with the protection that you wanted may be another matter entirely. It takes more than paperwork to establish a truly valid corporation capable of withstanding challenges that are apt to come when you need it most. The advice of a competent attorney is your best assurance of actually achieving that protection, if you elect to form a corporation. Competence is a key word here—an attorney who merely files what amounts to a kit on your behalf does you little service either—insist on candid advice on the formation of a corporation that will stand if challenged.

Perspective Is Required

There is something intoxicating about going into business for yourself. Among other important things, it's an ego trip; much of the motivation to endure the discomforts that sometimes precede the rewards comes from that ego strength. Just remember to keep your eye fixed on the primary objectives of survival, growth, and profitability as you start your business.

In the rush of getting organized, don't make it more complicated than it needs to be. There are good reasons for the more involved forms of structuring a business and some of them may apply to you. At least consider the possibility that the higher forms may be premature at the outset—depending on the scope of your business operations and, especially, its capitalization.

The popular (and often wise) practice of incorporating may be more trouble than it is worth for a small home-based business that doesn't have reasonably substantial assets. In such a case, the liability protection you *think* you have would probably not exist anyway, since a court would recognize the inadequacy of your capitalization and allow your personal assets to be seized. It might, however, still make sense from some tax perspective—so become well-informed, seek good counsel, and make your choice wisely.

Once you have the broad familiarity with the organizational options, you can pursue an intelligent choice. You will be better able to recognize when a certain form really makes sense for your home-based business. Avoid the rapture of sophisticated sounding moves that may best be left for a more mature stage of your company's development.

Awareness of the options should have you better prepared to seize dramatic tax savings and other corporate benefits when the time is right. Elect the *simplest* form of organization that meets your needs at a particular time in your business' development. Be prepared to move on to more advance forms as they are warranted and supported by your activity. Don't overlook the possibility that tax considerations will tip the balance in your attempt to reach a decision. Let your attorney and accountant assist you in optimizing the two key aspects of your organizational choice: (1) legal liability, and (2) tax consequences.

MANAGING YOUR BUSINESS (AND ITS OWNER)

You have selected your legal form of organization and it is time to address the day-to-day concerns of how you will actually operate. As a product of the traditional workplace, you may be better schooled and more experienced in the management of others than of self. Things are about to change for you as a home-based business person with a staff of none—or, at best, few.

MBO for One

If you worked as a manager in a large organization in the last 20 years, you had a brush with management by objectives—MBO. This simple and purposeful concept was made complex and ponderous by many a well-meaning manager. Too often it was a square to fill for a senior manager who asked a junior member of the team to make the necessary papers flow.

As a home-based businessperson with no one to cram it down your throat, you just might find a simplified form of MBO useful. The idea, with its formality removed, was essentially this:

- List your objectives.
- Prioritize them.
- Break them down into identifiable behaviors, so you will know when you have or have not done them.
- Set time limits for checking on your performance.
- Evaluate how you have done.
- Start all over again with new objectives that have been modified to accommodate what you have done and what remains—and with respect for changed conditions.

For some people such a process is as natural as getting out of bed in the morning, for some, it represents yet another ritual to leave behind at the traditional workplace. Certain people will find it something that they can usefully apply with varying degrees of formality in the operation of their home-based businesses.

MBO for one can be a highly personalized vestige of the corporate management mentality you left behind. It's like the amazement you experienced as the wisdom of your parents grew with your increasing years—some traditional thinking can actually be transplanted desirably to your newer, freer professional environment.

Whatever device you choose, goal setting, modification to changed conditions, and progress checks along the way, will be essential tools for building your success at a home office. No matter how informal, your business will need some form of planning and evaluation as it takes shape and grows. Popular management theories are some of the least original literature of our time, but useful for their reasoned statement of the obvious. If you don't already have a favorite to craft your personal self-management model after, a trip to the library or bookstore will offer you a variety of choices.

Motivation

If this *is* a problem, you *have* a problem. There is no place for low motivation in the home-based business that operates on the assumption that you are dealing with a labor of love that took you away from the traditional world of work and its extrinsic motivators.

Back when management began being treated as a science, we were given two ways to view human nature as it affected productivity in the workplace. Theory X said, in effect, that man was inherently lazy and needed to be driven to a state of productivity. Theory Y was for those who saw the basic tendency of workers to produce rather naturally, if they understood their work and had reasonable incentives—they really wanted to do a good job, given half a chance.

Theory X thinking won't work when the manager and the managed are the same person. You won't get much done by expecting the worst from yourself and administering self-punishment. Theory Y is the only way to go as a self-manager. You are the good guy, left to your own devices (you will be in a home-based business) and producing at the peak of your capabilities in the freedom of the home office.

For most home business operators, the immediacy of the financial realities will quickly resolve any motivational lapses. A business of your own should be something you enjoy. Paul Hawken (1987, p. 82) expressed it this way: "If you aren't having fun, you might wonder just what you are doing in your business life. Laughter and good humor are the canaries in the mine of commerce. If employees, customers, and vendors don't laugh and have a good time at your company, something is wrong." The same is true for you in the privacy of your home office —enjoy it, relish the challenge of another day of making things happen your way . . . or you are going to lose a lot of canaries.

Self-Discipline

Another given in home-based business is the ability to make yourself perform regularly and efficiently. Nonbusiness distractions abound, as do choices of less effective but more desirable ways to spend your limited professional time. The requirement to know what needs to be done and hold yourself to the very personal obligation of doing it, requires the kind of self-discipline that is nice to have, but less essential, outside the home-based business.

Division of Labor

Priorities are a must in your home office. You are the producer upon which the whole enterprise depends. There are things that you must do and others that you cannot afford to do yourself. Making those distinctions can mean the difference between success and failure in the home-based business. While you will probably not have a staff, at least in the early stages, you can purchase services to handle what you cannot and should not do yourself—if it would be at the expense of more profitable professional activities.

Profit Now Mentality

There are two points to understand when it comes to the question of profit and the home-based business. First, you make your profit by focused attention to the aspects of your business that have the most potential, and second, don't expect profit to materialize instantly and appear as regularly as the paycheck you may be accustomed to. If that is what you need, seriously consider starting your business on a part-time basis where cash flow and profit are not life and death items.

When to expect a profit? Paul Hawkin (1987, p. 128) says: "Forget about making money at first. Look at the first few months or year as tuition. If you do make money early, fine, but when you start a business, consider it a screaming success if it does not lose money." Your home-based business will have a little better chance of shortening the growth curve because of reduced expenses, but don't count on an instant, steady flow of income.

The profit *now* mentality is a reference to a way of thinking that you need to adopt to keep your priorities straight. There will be a cycle of activities in your business, whether it is video production or consulting. You will need to constantly choose the opportunity of the moment that offers the most immediate route to profit. If you are operating in one phase and see an opportunity to make money more quickly in another, the profit now mentality says shift gears at once and direct your efforts toward the highest profit potential. Your ability to change quickly will, of course, depend on the nature of your business. A major contracted project shouldn't to be set aside to seize another opportunity, but routine operations should be conducted with the expectation that priorities will shift to accommodate profit windows.

Pacing Yourself

Make your business something you can live with by knowing the scope of your commitments and being prepared to meet them with some degree of comfort. The pleasure and satisfaction that should be a part of a successful home business can pale in the light of unrealistic demands on your time and resources. Start at a level where reasonable people would expect you to succeed and grow.

An important advantage to having your office in your residence—and being the boss—is the freedom of deciding when to expend effort. Flex time (working hours that are not routine) is touted as a source of increased productivity in the traditional workplace, make it a part of your own scheduling. The pace you set can be a demanding one, and yet very tolerable, if it fits your newly combined life and work styles.

Criterion Referenced Rewards

Self-management calls for self-administered reinforcement for jobs well done. For your business to succeed, it will have to establish and reach milestones. As a one-person operation, the goals become personal and the criteria for meeting them are defined by your own behavior.

Trainers manage the progress of their students by defining precisely what the desired steps look like when they have been achieved. Some things lend themselves to such definition better than others. Never make such procedures a drudgery in the home office, but consider whether they can help you succeed. Here are some examples of how the technique might be applied at the home office:

- Consulting fee volume for the year is set at $100,000, if that figure is reached in October, you can literally give yourself the rest of the year off. "Off" might mean the relaxed pursuit of a lower priority, higher risk project or a vacation of indefinite length where the telephone and laptop computer keep you on top of your field, but at a relaxed pace.
- If you operate a business that can't be "turned down" the way consulting or other project oriented ones might be, your reward might take the form of new equipment or considering the addition of an associate or two to distribute the load when it rises above an acceptable benchmark.

Growing Pains

Any successful business crosses through some thresholds where it feels as though it is more trouble than it is worth. Expect this as you grow in your home-based business. Keep in mind that you are the person with the power to slow things down, if you find that the succeeding business is becoming more than you really want. It is extremely hard to look greater success in the eye and say "no thanks, I'll settle for less," but some people need to do exactly that.

If you are a manager as well as an accomplished person in your specialty, you may be pleasantly surprised at how rewarding and relatively easy it can be to grow without pain once you find yourself in demand. The secret is in managing everything from your own goals and the expenditure of your finite energies to the finances, personnel, and technological innovations that will probably accompany your growth.

CONCLUSION

The legal side of getting organized in the home-based business is solved relatively easily. The recommended rule of thumb is don't make it more complicated than it needs to be, but be aware of the possibilities and make changes as they are warranted. Personal organization and self-management is another issue and it falls on your shoulders more squarely than the legal decision that, once made, is largely implemented by your accountant and attorney. Self-management is largely a matter of personal style matched to the situation. If you find that you lack the skills to maintain the necessary order of things, get help for those areas and focus on the dollar-generating skills that you uniquely possess. Administrators are a dime-a-dozen, people with in-demand professional skills aren't.

Chapter 12

Satisfying the Regulators

There are people who are *very* interested in your home-based business. They are the dozens—perhaps hundreds—of government employees on every level from city hall to the federal building, from the state capital to the Washington bureaus whose Congressional mandates somehow touch whatever it is you do.

With few exceptions, these are right-hearted folks just doing a job and collecting a paycheck on their way to a pension. At the worst, they won't understand or care about what you are trying to accomplish, beyond collecting the requisite fees to perpetuate their offices. At the best, they can be positively helpful—well-informed and glad to steer you in the right direction. Many are in a position to see and know things that can present real obstacles in your path. By adopting the attitude that they are important sources of publicly funded help for your endeavor, there can be returns that far exceed the inconvenience and small expense usually associated with compliance. There are things you *cannot* do, unless you do them with the necessary approvals.

ZONING

Every organized community has, to a greater or a lesser extent, regulations that determine what sort of activities are permissible at the address you have chosen for your business. By definition, home-based businesses are in neighborhoods that are zoned residential. Residences may be in mixed use areas that will find little resistance to the addition of another business, or they may be in prestigious developments that might view the most unobtrusive consulting business as the first step in the demise of their residential enclave.

The less restrictive ordnances will say that yours is a residential address, but you can operate a business as long as it does not create a nuisance. From there the regulations escalate in severity through the need to apply for a variance before commencing operations, to the necessity of coming before a public hearing and justifying why you deserve to be the exception, or, if all else fails, petitioning a court for relief from unreasonable restrictions. Usually there is an appeal process that makes such drastic action unnecessary.

Generally the zoning laws will not present an insurmountable problem for the home-based business person. Many times the activity is begun informally as a part-time venture. By the time it reaches the point of attracting the attention of the zoning board, you are ready to make your case for being a nondisruptive addition to the residential neighborhood.

The regulators are used to a steady flow of people walking through their door with businesses to register that will almost certainly never see a renewal fee. Unless you are coming in with something that is going to create a hazard or get the neighbors upset over parking, noise, or a commercial sign that they consider a blight on the neighborhood, you will be allowed to put down your $25 fee and go about your business—until it comes back to them as a problem or complaint!

The home-based businessperson needs to approach the zoning board with a low profile, humble presentation of their business. The more it resembles an amateur exercise in entrepreneurship, the less threatening it will be. The zoning application is no place to tout your growth potential or potential client volume. Keep it simple and you will almost certainly have no problem in getting under way with the blessings of the local government.

Once you are inside the regulatory door and operating, the case for accommodating growth will be made more easily—the authorities and your neighbors will have experienced the low profile, nondisruptive nature of your home-based professional practice and accept it more readily.

In more complex zoning environments, you may have to coordinate the approvals of more than one office. Expect the business license issuer to have you pass through the office of the zoning czar and possibly others, if your activities would seem to pose any questions of public health or safety. This holds true for the apartment dweller in the heart of a major city as well as for the rural owner of a free-standing residence.

It weaves a web that you must work your way through. In metropolitan areas, for example, it is often convenient for a home-based business person from the suburbs of an adjoining state to maintain an apartment in the city for the purpose of doing business in that commercial center. A catch-22 situation arises—how can a *residential* apartment be the address for a *business* activity? Other regulations require the registration of the business—and you'd better do it if the business will have a profile high enough to be noticed.

The solution is obtaining what is known as a "franchise" license in the city. It establishes for the record and tax purposes, that a nonresident is operating a business in the city. A zoning variance is still necessary and will require some explanation. Don't be surprised if the only way that it can be granted is as a home-based business—which takes us back to the problem of that apartment not being your home!

Frustrating as they sound, such problems can be solved. Be prepared for a patient walk through the regulatory maze. Once you get it done, annual renewals should amount to nothing more complicated than paying the appropriate fees and not becoming the source of any complaints.

Private "Zoning"

If you reside in a condominium, cooperative, or other privately regulated community, be aware of possible restrictions. Your lease or ownership documents may limit the use of the property to a single-family residence. Common sense comes into play in most cases and if your home-based business is a discrete one, there will be no objections. The only reason for it to become an issue is if the community's approval is a necessary step in the governmental zoning process—much like the circular logic situation cited in case of the city "business" apartment that has to be a residence before it can qualify as a home-business zoning exception.

THE PART-TIME OFFICE OPTION

When all else fails, consider securing the least expensive lease you can get in a time-share office building. These are properly zoned commercial facilities complete with nonexclusive offices, conference rooms, and clerical services. You buy the right to use it on a periodic, rather than a daily basis. It is a more than satisfactory business address for your licensing and other regulatory requirements and may be the most hassle-free way around rules that don't fit your situation. Use of the mail handling and answering services alone will offset much of the lease. Access to copy services and the occasional need for a nonresidential conference setting can make it a worthy complement to your home-based business—or that supplementary city apartment for business purposes that can't otherwise be explained in some satisfactory way.

PROFESSIONAL LICENSES

Depending on your specialty, public agencies may regulate your activities by licensing your profession. While this sounds a bit obvious, you may be entering a field where no such regulations affected you while an organizational employee and they will when you set up a private practice. There may be tests, periods of supervision, or any of a number of other obstacles to screen the competency of the practitioners.

For most fields, the licensing requirements will be closely associated with the profession itself and a check with your private practice peers or national associations will put you in touch with the appropriate regulators. Where the lines are less clear, your state government will have an office dedicated to such matters and someone there will steer you to the relevant board.

In many fields, there is certification by national professional associations that complement the actual licensure needed to ply your trade in a given state. The insurance and real estate fields have their tests and certifications that vouch for competency in different specialties. Investment and data processing and other professions have study and supervised testing programs that qualify you for valuable letters to add to the business card and professional listings. Pursue them through your peers and associations, if you are not already aware of the institutes, federations, and so on that administer the certification programs, codes of ethical conduct, contracts, and other legal instruments that will set the standard in your practice.

TRADE LAWS

It is not likely that your home-based business will need to defend itself against interstate commerce infractions, restraint of trade, or unfair practices laws, but you should be aware of the potential. The most likely problem to arise would be an inadvertent run-in with the Federal Trade Commission (FTC) resulting from doing business across state lines. Even doing so doesn't do much more than subject you to their regulations, which you are not apt to violate. A complaint from a customer, competitor, or a neighbor who isn't happy with what you are doing in the neighborhood can cause you some grief. The FTC rules may give them the basis for having you cited.

SECURITIES LAWS

Raising money to fund the start up, expansion, or a particular project related to your home-based business can bring you fact-to-face with some of the most formidable regulations. The state corporation commission or attorney general's office can guide you to the applicable sections of the code and probably give you a quick briefing on the main problems to avoid. If you cross state lines to raise funds, you face even more demanding federal regulations.

Both the state and federal laws came into being to keep unscrupulous promoters from bilking naive investors with unwise, if not outright fraudulent, schemes. Be aware that this complex issue varies from state-to-state; you should seek legal advice before advertising for or publicly soliciting investors. Your activities must fit within strict guidelines that limit the number and kinds of investors.

PERMITS AND OTHER THINGS

While zoning and meeting the regulatory mandates of your profession are the main sources of concern as you set about establishing a home-based business, there are lesser things to note. Among them, permits.

Permits for the posting of signs and notices. Permits for the possession and storage of certain materials.

If you are in a business that involves hazardous materials or controlled substances, you will surely need to satisfy some associated regulations. The same would be true of anything that you might do to alter your residence's structure or wiring—building inspectors may have to give their blessings. Anytime these things cause bureaucrats to turn a page in the regulations that says "commercial" and you are operating in the home-based mode, expect to enter into a period of enlightened reasoning with them. There is something inherently contradictory between the two terms that raises red flags. They can be safely lowered, but keep in mind the wrath you may be inviting and avoid the issue if possible. Your time is better spent elsewhere!

DON'T WORRY, THEY'LL FIND YOU!

Unless you are really blatant about it, it is no great sin to fail to uncover every last possibility in the regulatory chain. Make a good faith effort to get your home-based business appropriately licensed and see to it that you accommodate the zoning necessities—and by all means have your business on record as properly meeting every tax obligation of which you are aware.

With that done, relax and go about your principal task of making money. Cross checks, formal and informal, exist that will fill in the blanks if you have inadvertently overlooked anyone. If an imposing officious letter arrives in the mail, respond in a timely and positive manner—in person, if the office is within easy access. Demonstrate your good faith by showing all of the things you have done to get started on the right foot and express your appreciation for their efforts to bring their services to your attention. Pay the tax or fee and get on with your money-making activities.

Chapter 13

Tax Obligations and Opportunities to Save

There are special considerations to keep in mind if you are to take advantage of the lucrative tax breaks that await you as a home-based businessperson, and still avoid costly difficulties with the tax authorities. Many perfectly legitimate opportunities exist for you to claim substantial relief from your tax obligations on the basis of home-based business expenses, deductions, and credits. However, tax administrators are strict in their oversight of these provisions—you will have to know what you are doing.

POTENTIAL HOME BUSINESS TAX SAVINGS

- *Home Office*
  Mortgage interest
  Depreciation
  Rent
  Maintenance and repairs
  Taxes
  Cleaning
  Decorating

- *General Business Expenses*

  Telephone

  Utilities

  Postage

  Depreciation of furnishing, fixtures, and equipment

  Business use of car

  Travel and entertainment

  Wages and fees for services paid to others

  Leased furnishing, fixtures, and equipment

- *Retirement Plan Contributions*

  Keogh, HR-10

  SEP

These and other tax-favored home-based business expenses are discussed in this chapter. The IRS forms used in the administration of these regulations are found in *Tax Guide for Small Business*. You may want to obtain a copy and refer to these actual forms and examples as you encounter discussions of them in coming sections of the book.

Congress views small business as a good thing that deserves financial encouragement under the tax codes, but it is very sensitive to abuse. The Internal Revenue Service's Schedule C (Form 1040) is the one most commonly used by home-based businesses reporting their income. The eighth entry on that 42-item form asks: "Are you deducting expenses for an office in your home? (If 'Yes,' see instruction for specific limitations)." The same federal hand that reaches out to assist the small businessperson stands ready to check closely on adherence to the rules that go with the breaks.

Expect ambivalence as you try to find a balance between tax paranoia that leaves you afraid to pursue the relief you deserve and unreasonable avoidance that can land you in a lot of trouble. You are entitled to every *allowable* expense, credit, or deduction and will have a better chance of succeeding financially in your business if you identify and take them, but you must be ready to answer to a skeptical review by those who administer the programs.

The material in this chapter heightens your awareness of potential home-based business tax savings. It *does not* replace essential professional advice focused on your unique circumstances. Anticipate that expense; taxation is a detailed, specialized, and constantly changing field in which you are unlikely to stay proficient as an amateur. When it comes time for an audit—always a strong possibility as a home-based professional whose patterns of income and expenses will vary from those of the "typical taxpayer"—you will want to know that you have made your claims correctly and that they can be defended.

TAX SAVINGS FOR THE HOME-BASED BUSINESS

As you try to find your potential tax breaks and obligations, you will first have to categorize your home-based business on several criteria. This chapter leads you through the possibilities, including the high probability that you are neither fish nor fowl in some important areas. Judgment, balance, and sufficient awareness to sort through the situation with your professional tax adviser is what is called for—begin with a view of your overall picture.

Is Your Home Office Deductible?

You will be treated differently for tax purposes depending on how you fit into the possible patterns of people working from their homes. As summarized in the February 1989 edition of *Money* magazine, to qualify as a write-off:

1. Your home office must be used for work exclusively and on a regular basis *and*
2. You must either run your own business out of it, regularly see clients or patients there, *or* do work there that is required by your employer and justified by the nature of your job.

You can then deduct:

1. A percentage of your home mortgage interest, house insurance, and utilities *and*
2. The full amount of office and business costs *and*
3. Depreciation of the office itself and your equipment.

Unless you are using the office as a requirement of your employer. Then you can deduct only the amount by which your allowable expenses exceed 2 percent of your adjusted gross income. (Adapted from Hedberg, 1989, p. 44.)

You need to know more about each of these topics to determine exactly what tax benefits you qualify for.

Employee or Self-Employed? It matters whether you are on someone else's payroll and claiming expenses for work you *do at home* for that employer or working for yourself and claiming the costs of work done at home—either full or part time.

- *Is the home office required?* If you are working for someone else, it will be necessary to establish that you are working at home for the convenience of your employer (inadequate work space at your primary place of business or some other compelling reason why the tasks could not be done in space already provided by the employer). The self-employed person faces no such test, because there is no employer provided work space.

- *Principal place of business activity.* An employee will find it very difficult to establish that the focal point of his or her work is anywhere but the space provided by an employer. If you are *self-employed* and your principal place of business for a particular profit-making activity is your home, there is no question on this criterion.

- *Full or a qualified deduction.* If you are an employee, your home business expenses are deductible as another miscellaneous itemized deduction on Schedule A and subject to the 2 percent (of Adjusted Gross Income) floor on those combined deductions. A self-employed home worker avoids this problem by using Schedule C on which any legitimate expense of the business is fully deductible.

Just because you still draw a paycheck somewhere doesn't mean that your separate home-based business cannot qualify for tax treatment as that of a self-employed person. A secondary or sideline business qualifies—the trick is to draw a clear distinction between it and what you do as an employee of someone else. Keep in mind that the home office deduction for such a sideline cannot exceed its gross income, but there are carry-over provisions worth investigating. They may make these losses fully deductible over the course of future, more profitable years.

Regular and Exclusive Use A major test of the legitimacy of your home office is whether it can be defined as a space that is clearly delineated from those parts of your residence used for other purposes and whether it gets regular business use.

- *Physical separation.* While desirable, it is not really necessary that your home office be a specific room set aside from other functions of the residence. No physical barrier is required, if the functional ones are apparent.
- *Exclusive use.* You can't maintain that a recreation room, for example, has a dual purpose as both a home office and a center for family activities. You can designate part of that room as your place of business and convincingly establish that it gets no other use.
- *Regular use.* Exclusive use is no substitute for regular use. Incidental or occasional use will not qualify. The home office must be the place where your business is conducted.

Rent or Own You don't have to be a home *owner* to qualify for home-based business privileges, but what can be considered deductible expenses will vary considerably.

- *Deductions for a renter or home owner.* The *renter* is entitled to deduct a pro rata share of the rent and associated expenses paid on the part of a residence used for business. The *home owner* can deduct a pro rata share of the allowable expenses associated with the purchase, operation, and maintenance of a home— based on the amount of space used for the business. Just as home ownership is the single largest tax shelter for most ordinary citizens, it is also the source for some of the most generous deductions for your home business. These can include depreciation, painting the exterior, general repairs, extermination and termite inspections, mortgage interest, and property taxes (*1989 Tax Guide for College Teachers*, p. 62).

  Owners and renters qualify for the business' share of such things as utilities, cleaning costs, insurance, painting the office space, and so on. Refer to the "Worksheet for Figuring the Deduction for Business Use of a Home" in the IRS Publication 587, *Business Use of Your Home,* for a systematic examination of the deductions apt to be available to you.

Figure 13-1 is the IRS's worksheet for calculating the amount of home office business deduction to which you may be entitled.

Worksheet for Figuring the Deduction for Business Use of a Home

Step 1—Part of your home used for business:

Part A. Area basis (part used exclusively)

    1) Area of home used for business   1)_____
    2) Total area of home   2)_____
    3) Percentage of home used for business (divide line 1 by line 2)   3)_____

Part B. Time usage basis (part used to provide day-care services)

    4) Total hours facility used (days x   hrs)   4)_____
    5) Total hours available (24 hrs. x 366 days)   5) 8784
    6) Percentage of time used for business (divide line 4 by line 5)   6)_____
    7) Percentage of home used for business (multiply line 6 by line 3)   7)_____

Step 2—Figuring your gross income limit:

    8a) Gross receipts from business use of your home: 8a)_____
    b) Less returns and allowances   8b)_____
    c) Less cost of goods sold   8c)_____
    9) **Gross income from business**   9)_____
    10) Enter in **Business part** the **Total expenses** multiplied by the business percentage as figured in a reasonable allocation such as line 3 or line 7, if applicable:

	Total expense	Business part
a) Deductible mortgage interest	10a)_____	_____
b) Real estate taxes	10b)_____	_____
c) Casualty losses	10c)_____	_____

    d) Total of (a) through (c). Subtract line 10(d) from line 9, but do not enter less than zero (–0–)   10d)_____
    e) **Balance**   10e)_____
    11) Less other business expenses not attributable to unit (salaries, business phone, etc.)   11)_____
    12) **Gross income limit** (but not less than zero)   12)_____

Step 3—Business part of expenses attributable to the unit

    13) Enter in **Business part** the **Total expenses** multiplied by the business percentage as figured in a reasonable allocation such as line 3 or line 7, if applicable:

	Total expense	Business part
a) Utilities	13a)_____	_____
b) Insurance	13b)_____	_____
c) Maintenance	13c)_____	_____
d) Repairs	13d)_____	_____
e) Excess mortgage interest	13e)_____	_____
f) Other expenses	13f)_____	_____

    g) Total of (a) through (f), plus carryover from last year   13g)_____

If line 13(g) is equal to or less than line 12, subtract line 13(g) from line 12, enter the balance here, and go on to Step 4. If line 12 is zero, enter -0- on line 13(h) and carry over the excess on line 13(g), along with any excess amount in Step 4, to next year. If line 13(g) exceeds line 12, deduct only those expenses equal to line 12. You must carry over the excess expense to next year, along with any excess from Step 4. **Balance** (if any)[1]

    13h)_____

Step 4—Depreciation and excess casualty loss

    14) Excess casualty loss ($100 plus 10% of your adjusted gross income)   14)_____
    15) Figuring depreciation for your home (use Form 4562 or the table below)[2]:
        a) Adjusted basis of home   15a)_____
        b) Less—land   15b)_____
        c) Basis of building   15c)_____
        d) Business percentage (line 3 or line 7, above, whichever applies)   15d)_____
        e) **Business** basis of building (multiply line (c) by line (d))   15e)_____
        f) ACRS (or MACRS) percentage or other method of depreciation   15f)_____
        g) Depreciation allowable (multiply line (e) by line (f)), or from Form 4562, plus last year's carryover   15g)_____

Add lines 14 and 15(g) and enter the total on line 15(h). If line 15(h) is equal to or less than line 13(h), deduct line 15(h) from line 13(h) and enter the balance here. If line 15(h) exceeds line 13(h), deduct only an amount equal to line 13(h). You must carry over the excess to next year.[1]

    15h)_____
    15i)_____

[1] Any excess amount on lines 13(g) and 15(h) carried over to next year is subject to the gross income limit (line 12 of worksheet) for that year.

[2] See Publication 534, *Depreciation,* for more information on figuring depreciation.

Figure 13-1 IRS worksheet for figuring your home office deduction. (Source: Internal Revenue Service Publication 587, *Business Use of Your Home,* revised November 1988)

Residential and Business Use?   The home office limitations apply only to properties used *both* as a residence and a business. If you maintain a separate property—an apartment in the city—and it is totally for business purposes, you are not faced with these tests and limitations (although you must be prepared to defend its exclusive use as a business property and not a second home). If your business is a separate part of your residential property, however—perhaps an old carriage house that has been converted into a studio—you better be prepared to meet the tests associated with home office expenses, although it may be more easily done.

Demonstrated Profit Motive/Hobby Loss   It is easy to qualify for paying taxes, but deducting losses from the operation of a business can be more difficult. In order to qualify for the latter, you must be judged to be in a business and not a hobby. Should you find yourself classified as a hobby, any profits will be taxed, but expenses exceeding the business' income will not be deductible—no losses are allowed.

You must be seriously engaged in the pursuit of profit, not merely satisfying your ego. Since December 31, 1986, you have to show a profit in three of five consecutive tax years to satisfy what is known as the "presumption of profit-seeking." Prior to that time, the test was met by having two profitable years out of five. This is only a rule-of-thumb, however; and you must be prepared to demonstrate convincingly that you are committed to a serious money-making venture. It is possible to make an election with the IRS that postpones the profit motive determination for four years from your business start up, if you expect to show losses in the early years. That is accomplished by filing a Form 5213.

The Expenses Only Option   Another possibility to keep in mind is that your home office can be disallowed and the business expenses incurred there found to be acceptable deductions. At some point in the evolution of your home-based business, you may find it an unnecessary burden to establish and defend a home office. It may be more prudent to devote your energies to operating your business in circumstances that are comfortable to your lifestyle, without regard to the strict rules of the IRS. In such cases, you are perfectly within your rights to deduct the costs of supplies, services, and other reasonable expenses associated with doing business at home. Another position is for you to claim the home office in good faith, but keep "business expenses only" as a fall back position to take if the office itself is denied.

Things You Can't Deduct The IRS is constantly identifying and plugging loopholes in its regulations. Here are a few loopholes that have become history and should be avoided:

- *Renting to your employer.* One of the popular ruses for getting around meeting the home office test was the practice of renting that home office space to your employer. The 1986 Tax Reform Act took care of that. Neither does it help to qualify as an independent contractor and rent the space to those hiring you for services—even though you are not technically their employee.

- *Investment management.* If you are relying on help from your investment activities in rounding out the case for an acceptable home office, keep this in mind: The only way to qualify your investment activities for a home office deduction now is to be an active short-term trader. Supporting your long-term investments by reading, research, and so forth won't satisfy the necessary requirement that your investment interests constitute a trade or business (*Tax Guide for College Teachers*, p. 58).

- *Residential telephone.* After tax year 1988, it is no longer possible to deduct a percentage of the cost of local telephone service for the *first* phone line into your house. You can do so for long distance charges and optional services such as call waiting placed on that line, but installing additional lines is the only way to claim the business use of local service and the taxes (*Prentice Hall's Explanation of the Technical and Miscellaneous Revenue Act of 1988*, p. 16).

LEGAL FORM OF ORGANIZATION AND TAX SAVINGS

In the *Tax Guide for Small Business* (1988, p. 5), the IRS advises that you must decide what type of business entity to use when you start a business. The normal choices are the sole proprietorship, partnership, or corporation, and there are important tax consequences associated with each. Briefly, sole proprietorships and partnerships pay no taxes as organizations, since the proprietors or partners include the profits or losses on their personal income tax returns. Except for the S corporation, profits from a corporation are taxed as corporate profits and, again, individually as shareholder dividends.

Sole Proprietor Taxes

Sole proprietorships are the simplest form of business organization. The same is true for taxation—the profits or losses of the business are your own and you deal with them directly on your personal tax forms. The following information is abstracted from the *Tax Guide for Small Business* (1988, p. 5):

> **Profit or loss.** When you figure your taxable income for the year, you must add in any profit, or subtract out any loss, you have from your sole proprietorship. You must report the profit or loss from each of your businesses operated as a sole proprietorship on a separate Schedule C (Form 1040) *Profit or Loss From Business*. The amount of this business profit or loss is entered as an item of profit or loss on your individual income tax return Form 1040.
>
> If you are a sole proprietor, you are probably liable for self-employment tax. You ordinarily will have to make estimated tax payments.
>
> *Assets.* Each asset in your sole proprietorship is treated separately for tax purposes, rather than as part of one overall ownership interest. For example, a sole proprietor selling an entire business as a going concern figures gain or loss separately on each asset.

Partnership Taxes

The next level of organizational complexity is the partnership, which is a form of shared individual ownership. The following information is abstracted from the *Tax Guide for Small Business* (1988, p. 5):

> A partnership is not a taxable entity. However, it must figure its profit or loss and file a return. A partnership files its return on Form 1065, *U.S. Partnership Return of Income*.
>
> For income tax purposes, the term partnership includes a syndicate, group, pool, joint venture, or other unincorporated organization that is carrying on a business and that may not be classified as a trust, estate, or

corporation. The partnership agreement is generally the basis for determining a partner's share of income, gain, loss, deductions, or credits. A partner's income tax for the year is paid on his own individual income tax return and is based on his distributive share of partnership gains and losses and other matters effecting taxation such as charitable contributions and depletion allowances, if applicable. The partner is subject to self-employment tax and most of the withholding obligations of the sole proprietor.

Corporation Taxes

There are two principal types of corporations that would be of potential interest to a home-based business owner. The regular C Corporation which is the structure used by major companies having no interest in the owners retaining any benefits of taxation as individuals and the S corporation (or Subchapter S Corporation) which is a device for treating corporate income and losses much like those of an individual. It does away with the dual taxation experienced when income is taxed both as earnings of the corporation and again as dividends paid to individual stockholders.

Here is an example of what that might mean for a relatively small corporation (adapted from Diamond & Williams, 1987, p. 104). A change from the regular corporate organization to that of an S *corporation reduced the owner's net income taxes by over 16 percent* in this case:

- Regular C Corporation

  Taxable corporate income of $20,000 for the year

  Taxed at the 15% corporate rate (15% of $20,000 = $3000)

  A single shareholder employee who is paid a salary of $20,000 a year and dividends of the $17,000 remaining to be distributed after the corporate tax of $3000

  For simplicity sake, we tax her combined income of $37,000 at the 28% tax rate and she pays $10,360 personally.

  Corporate $3000 + $10,360 personal = $13,360 total tax paid.

- S Corporation

  No corporate tax

  Full $20,000 of corporate income passed through to employee shareholder for a total personal income of $40,000

  Personal tax on $40,000 = $11,200

  $2,160 saved in total taxes ($13,360 − $11,200 = $2,160).

Goldstein (1988, p. 8) shows more dramatic savings for a higher earning small corporation that could very well have been a home-based business. His example assumes corporate income of $100,000 which would be taxed $22,250 as a C Corporation. The remaining $77,750 becomes dividend income to the shareholder and his wife who then pay $22,073 in personal income taxes—a total of $44,323, or nearly 45 cents on the dollar! The same scenario in an S Corporation finds the full $100,000 passed through to the shareholder for personal tax treatment resulting in an assessment of $28,293—*a total tax savings of about $16,000—or 36%!*

These examples demonstrate why the S Corporation is the darling of the small business owner. Foth and Englebrecht (1984, p. 511) summarize the tax advantage as follows:

The rationale for Subchapter S, that businesses should have the freedom to choose their legal form of organization on the basis of business considerations without the influence of income tax consequences, has long enjoyed substantial popular support. This view recognizes that, where businesses possess essentially similar economic characteristics and operational relationships, such businesses should receive comparable treatment under the income tax laws. This concept, as currently reflected in Subchapter S of the Internal Revenue Code, permits shareholders of closely held corporations to be taxed as though they were carrying on their activities as partners. Thus, under certain circumstances, shareholders may elect to be taxed directly on corporate earnings in lieu of imposition of any tax at the corporate level.

The S corporation retains many of the traditional advantages of incorporation (see Chapter 11), in addition to being taxed essentially as an individual or a partnership. When your home-based business is sufficiently capitalized and productive to justify it, plan to discuss S corporation status with your accountant and attorney. There are cautions as well as advantages, J. K. *Lasser's Your Income Tax 1989* (p. 184) indicates that the S corporation election is generally a reasonable one when:

- Your personal tax rates do not exceed the corporate tax rates.
- You cannot take sufficient money out of a corporation without subjecting some or all of it to the double tax.
- Special considerations such as passing early year losses on to stockholders with other income to offset them.

Election and management of an S corporation is sufficiently complex that it should be approached with the assistance of an income tax professional.

OTHER HOME-BASED BUSINESS TAXPAYER TIPS

In addition to determining under which circumstances your home office qualifies for tax savings and how to benefit from the best form of business organization, there are other tax terms, topics, obligations, and savings opportunities that a home-based business person should be aware of.

Family Members on the Payroll

Julian Block (1988) pointed out in the October 1988 *Home BusinessLine* that there can be advantages in paying a child a reasonable wage for actual work done in a home-based business. Changes in the tax law have severely limited other ways to convey gifts and investments to children, but wages remain deductible to the business. It represents one of the few remaining ways to benefit from the child's lower tax bracket.

In 1988, a child was entitled to a standard deduction of $3000 for income from wages, a figure that is expected to go higher in later years. There is also a special exemption from payroll taxes for family businesses that are not corporations. Block (1988) offered this illustration of how the family deduction could benefit a home-based business person:

> During 1988, you pay $3000 to a teenage son to make deliveries or to do clerical work for your home-based business. You fall into a 35% Federal and state bracket, whereas your child's wages escape taxes because of the standard deduction. The savings is $1050 or almost $825, if . . . the wages are subject to Social Security taxes.
>
> Caution: For this income-shifting device to survive an IRS audit, you must be able to establish that your children actually render services. Moreover, the wages that you pay them must be "reasonable," that is, not more than the going rate for unrelated employees who perform comparable tasks. (pp. 1 and 8)

Taxpayer Identification Number

If you are a sole proprietorship, you generally use your social security number as your taxpayer identification number. Put it on each of your individual tax forms, such as Form 1040 and the relevant schedules. Partnerships and corporations, including S corporations, must have an employer identification number (EIN) to use as their taxpayer identification numbers. Sole proprietors only need EINs when they:

- Pay wages to one or more employees or
- Must file any pension or excise tax returns.

Be alert to the following changes that could obligate you to get a new EIN:

- A sole proprietorship incorporates
- A sole proprietorship takes in partners and operates as a partnership
- A partnership incorporates
- A partnership is taken over by one of the partners and is operated as a sole proprietorship
- A corporation changes to a partnership or to a sole proprietorship.

Reporting Income and Claiming Deductions

The general rules for reporting business or professional income or losses are summarized in Figure 13-2. You should file a separate Schedule C along with Form 1040, if you are

- a sole proprietor of a business;
- a professional in your own practice.

Even if you do not fit into the above classes, report on Schedule C any self-employment income, such as income from a sideline business. Do not file Schedule C if your business is operated through a partnership or corporation.

Net business profit (or loss) figured on Schedule C is entered on . . . Form 1040. Thus, business profit (or loss) is added to (or subtracted

GENERAL REPORTING RULES ¶5.1

Guide to Reporting Business and Professional Income and Loss

Item	Comment
Tax return to file	If you are self-employed, prepare Schedule C to report business or professional income. If you are a farmer, use Schedule F. You attach Schedule C and/or F to Form 1040. If you operate as a partnership use Form 1065; if you operate in a corporation, Form 1120S or Form 1120.
Method of reporting income	The cash or accrual accounting rules determine when you report income and expenses. You must use the accrual basis if you sell a product that must be inventoried. The cash and accrual basis methods are discussed at ¶5.2.
Tax reporting year	There are two general tax reporting years: calendar years which end on December 31; and fiscal years which end on the last day of any month other than December. Your taxable year must be the same for both your business and nonbusiness income. Most business income must be reported on a calendar year. If, as a self-employed person, you report your business income on a fiscal year basis, you must also report your nonbusiness income on a fiscal year basis. Use of fiscal years is restricted as explained in Chapter 10.
Office in home	To claim home office expenses as a self-employed person, you must prove that you use the home area exclusively and on a regular basis either as a place of business to meet or deal with patients, clients, or customers in the normal course of your business or as your principal place of business; see ¶5.11.
Social Security coverage	If you have self-employed income, you may have to pay self-employment tax which goes to financing social security benefits; see ¶5.51
Passive participation in a business	If you do not regularly, continuously, and substantially participate in the business, your business income or loss is subject to passive activity restrictions. A loss is deductible only against other passive activity income. The passive activity restrictions are discussed in detail in Chapter 11.
Self-employed Keogh plan	You may set up a retirement plan based on business or professional income. If you are self-employed you may contribute to a self-employed retirement plan according to rules of ¶8.13.
Depreciation	Business assets other than real estate placed in service in 1988 are depreciable over 3, 5, 7, 10, 15, or 20 years. Automobiles and light trucks, computers and office equipment are in the five-year class. Property in the 3-, 5-,7-, and 10-year classes are depreciable using the double declining balance method, switching to the straight line method so as to maximize the deduction. See ¶5.22 for details on depreciation. Instead of depreciating equipment, you may claim the first-year expensing deduction. You may generally deduct up to $10,000 in 1988.
Health insurance	If you are self-employed, you may deduct in 1988 and 1989, 25% of the amounts paid for health insurance on behalf of yourself, your spouse, and dependents. The deduction may not exceed your net earnings from the business for which the health plan is established. You may not claim the deduction if you have employee coverage under another plan or coverage under your spouse's employer plan. If you have employees, they must generally be covered under nondiscrimination rules. The deduction is allowed as an adjustment to income on Line 26 of Form 1040 whether or not you claim itemized deductions.
Net operating losses	A loss incurred in your profession or business is deducted from other income reported on Form 1040. If the 1988 loss (plus any casualty loss) exceeds income, the excess may be first carried back to 1985, 1986, 1987, and then forward 15 years to 1989 through 2003 until it is used up. A loss carried back to a prior year reduces income of that year and entitles you to a refund. A loss applied to a later year reduces income for that year. You may elect to carry forward your loss for 15 years, forgoing the three-year carryback; see ¶5.21.
Sideline business	You report business income of a sideline business following the rules that apply to full-time business. For example, if you are self-employed, you report business income on Schedule C. You may also have to pay self-employment tax on this income. You may also set up a self-employment retirement plan based on such income. If you incur losses over several years, the hobby loss rules of ¶5.9 may limit your loss deduction.

Figure 13–2 Summary of reporting rules (note that references are to parts of the source book). (From the book, *J. K. Lasser's Your Income Tax 1989*, prepared by J. K. Lasser Institute, © 1988. Used by permission of the publisher, J. K. Lasser Institute, New York, NY)

from) non-business income on Form 1040. This procedure gives you the chance to deduct your business expenses, whether or not you claim itemized deductions.

On Schedule C, you deduct all of your business expenses from your business income. Then after adding your business profit to, or subtracting a business loss from non-business income on Form 1040, you may itemize non-business deductions on Schedule A, such as charitable contributions, taxes, and medical expenses—provided the total of itemized deductions exceeds the standard deduction.

Business persons and professionals may get a refund of taxes paid in three prior tax years, if current business losses exceed present income. If the loss is not fully eliminated by the income of the three prior years, the balance of the loss may be used to reduce income of 15 following years (*J. K. Lasser's Your Income Tax 1989* p. 74).

These reporting rules and procedures form the basis for benefiting from having a home-based business. When all of the bells and whistles are taken away, the main device for realizing a tax gain on the operation of your business is having a legitimate way to write off your costs of doing business.

There are tax consequences for almost any move you make as a home-based businessperson. The basic reasoning that you should pursue in deciding whether an expense might result in a tax saving has two components. First, is the item a reasonable and necessary expense that contributes to the operation of your business? Second, how should the cost be fairly prorated between your normal home expenses and those of the business activity? From that point on, check the tax regulations carefully for how all sorts of special situations are handled or turn the list over to your professional tax adviser for proper treatment under the current rules.

Recordkeeping

The *Tax Guide for Small Business* (1988, pp. 6–8) spells out in detail what is expected in terms of records required to substantiate your tax claims. The general requirement is as follows:

You must keep records to correctly figure your taxes. The *Checklist* . . . [Figure 13–3] lists the due dates of various taxes that might apply to your business. Your records must be permanent, accurate, complete, and must clearly establish your income, deductions, credits, and employee information. The law does not require you to keep your records in any particular way. But if you have more than one business, you should keep a complete and separate set of books and records for each business.

You are required to substantiate your expenses for travel including local travel, gifts, entertainment, and the business use of certain property, with adequate records or sufficient evidence to prove your own statements. Adequate records include account books, diaries, trip sheets, or similar items. Records that are written at or near the time you have the expenses are better evidence than oral statements or written records reconstructed much later.

Whether or not the items in Figure 13-3 apply depends on your form of legal organization, whether you have employees, and whether your business is engaged in the kind of activity that requires the payment of such things as excise taxes.

Keep the necessary records to meet your obligations and qualify for deserved tax breaks, but make it as simple as possible. The finest set of books in the world won't keep you in business if the bottom line doesn't show a profit. That accrues to hard, smart work that will bring in the dollars to pay for other people to worry about the fine points of the records. These points were abstracted from the *Tax Guide for Small Business* (1988, pp. 6–8) publication for your general guidance:

- Choose an accounting method (cash or accrual) and a tax year (fiscal or calendar year).
- Choose a bookkeeping system (single or double entry).
- Set up a separate business checking account and use it as a means of documenting all business income and expenses.
- Save receipts and other records to support your entries.
- Classify your accounts into income, expenses, assets, liabilities, and equity (net worth).
- Keep your books and records available for inspection for as long as they may be needed in the administration of any IRS law (technically, that's 3 years from the date the return was due, but there are circumstances where that statute of limitations does not apply, including allegations of fraud—so plan to keep your records indefinitely).

You may be liable for	If you are:	Use Form	Due on or before
Income tax	Sole proprietor	Schedule C (Form 1040)	Same day as Form 1040
	Individual who is a partner or S corporation shareholder	1040	15th day of 4th month after end of tax year
	Corporation	1120 or 1120–A	15th day of 3rd month after end of tax year
	S corporation	1120S	15th day of 3rd month after end of tax year
Self-employment tax	Sole proprietor, or individual who is a partner	Schedule SE (Form 1040)	Same day as Form 1040
Estimated tax	Sole proprietor, or individual who is a partner or S corporation shareholder	1040–ES	15th day of 4th, 6th, and 9th months of tax year, and 15th day of 1st month after the end of tax year
	Corporation	1120–W	15th day of 4th, 6th, 9th and 12th months of tax year
Annual return of income	Partnership	1065	15th day of 4th month after end of tax year
Social security (FICA) tax and the withholding of income tax	Sole proprietor, corporation, S corporation, or partnership	941	4–30, 7–31, 10–31, and 1–31
		8109 (to make deposits)	See Chapter 33
Providing information on social security (FICA) tax and the withholding of income tax	Sole proprietor, corporation, S corporation, or partnership	W–2 (to employee)	1–31
		W–2 and W–3 (to the Social Security Administration)	Last day of February
Federal unemployment (FUTA) tax	Sole proprietor, corporation, S corporation, or partnership	940	1–31
		8109 (to make deposits)	4–30, 7–31, 10–31, and 1–31, but only if the liability for unpaid tax is more than $100
Information returns for payments to nonemployees and transactions with other persons	Sole proprietor, corporation, S corporation, or partnership	See Chapter 36	Forms 1099—to the recipient by 1–31 and to the Internal Revenue Service by 2–28 Other forms —see Chapter 36
Excise taxes	Sole proprietor, corporation, S corporation, or partnership	See Chapter 35	See the instructions to the forms

Figure 13–3 IRS table of business reporting obligations. (Source: Internal Revenue Service Publication 334, *Tax Guide for Small Business,* revised November 1988)

- If you are an employer, expect to keep extensive records relating to income tax withholding, social security taxes, and federal unemployment taxes.

Estimated Tax

This is the method used to collect taxes on income not subject to withholding—and that includes income from self-employment. If you are also working as an employee and having tax withheld, you will have to determine whether it is enough to meet the tax obligations of both your employer paid and self-employed incomes. If not, you must pay additional estimated tax. Failure to pay by the dates due (usually quarterly) can result in penalties. Generally, you should make estimated tax payments if you figure that your tax for the coming year will be $500 or more and you estimate that the total amount of income tax withheld and your credits will be less than the lesser of:

- 90 percent of the tax to be shown on your next income tax return, or
- 100 percent of the tax shown on your present income tax return, if it covered all 12 months.

Generally, it is safe to assume that if you withhold at least as much as you owed in taxes for the last year, you will be protected from penalties. All of this can get complicated, so check *Tax Withholding and Estimated Tax*, Publication 505 of the IRS, or confer with your tax consultant.

Self-Employment Tax

You have an obligation to pay Social Security tax on the first $45,000 of your income in 1988 ($48,000 in 1989). If you work for an employer and the tax is withheld, you are probably covered by that withholding, if your wages meet at least the dollar amounts noted. If you are totally self-employed, you must pay the tax along with your estimated tax as self-employed tax at a rate of 13.02 percent. Employed wages of less than the totals mentioned obligate you to make up the difference with the self-employment tax.

Retirement Plans

Retirement is treated differently under the tax laws based on whether you are an employee or are self-employed. To accommodate the retirement needs of self-employed people, the IRS allows them to be treated as though they were employees for this special purpose.

Self-employed retirement plans, also known as Keogh or HR-10 plans, are available to sole proprietors and partnerships under a special rule that permits them to be treated as employees. The effect of the law is to provide a tax incentive to make contributions toward the future retirement of yourself and any employees you may have. The IRS has a worksheet for calculating the exact deduction that you are allowed, but the overall parameters are that a sole proprietor or a partner may deduct contributions to a Keogh profit-sharing plan of up to $30,000 or 15 percent of compensation from the trade or business, whichever is less. It gets involved—the plan must be IRS approved, and so on—insurance companies and financial institutions have preapproved plans that are available. You can also set up such a plan based on the earnings of a sideline business, even though you are covered by an employer's plan.

Another tax-advantaged approach to accumulating retirement benefits is the Simplified Employee Pension (SEP). It provides a way for the employer to contribute up to $30,000 or 15 percent of an employee's compensation, whichever is less, to an IRA or annuity. Again, the sole proprietor or partner is treated as an employee for this purpose.

Computer Deductions

The rules for writing off the cost of a computer, as of the 1988 tax year, are difficult for employees working at home. It must be required and not an optional piece of equipment—much as home office space must be for the convenience of the employer. A 50 percent business use test must also be met. A self-employed person faces the same 50 percent text, but it " . . . does not apply to computers used exclusively in a business establishment that you operate. A home office qualifying under the rules . . . is treated as a business establishment." (*J.K. Lasser's Your Income Tax 1989*, p. 91)

Expensing vs. Deducting

Qualifying business property can always be depreciated over the period of its useful life and a certain amount claimed as an expense (depreciation) in each of those years. There is a more straight forward way of claiming the deduction for your business property purchases, if they did not exceed $10,000. Within certain limitations, such as not exceeding the businesses taxable income for the year, you can elect to "expense" the property and take it all in the first year, instead of getting involved in the process of setting up a depreciation schedule and stretching it out over a period of years. It is known as the Section 179 deduction.

Section 1244 Stock

Just as the S corporation provides an organizational form that allows for corporate income and losses to be passed through to the personal income taxes of the shareholders, Section 1244 stock allows corporate losses to be treated as ordinary income, rather than capital losses. It is a means for small businesses to use the corporate form of organization and still more favorable tax treatment on its losses, if they occur. Section 1244 stock is limited to small corporations that meet certain tests.

TAX FORMS OF INTEREST TO THE HOME-BASED BUSINESS PERSON

While tax forms change from year-to-year, they contain essentially the same information. A review of those applicable to your situation can be helpful in your planning.

There are many aspects of taxation that also relate to matters of regulation and legal organization. Other chapters of this book address those issues in greater detail and you should review them. Chapter 11 provides you with additional information on legal forms of business organization. Chapter 12 explains zoning, licensing, and other things that may have ramifications for your taxes. Many local fees are nothing more than taxes in another form and just as important to satisfy.

CONCLUSION

Taxation is at once the biggest headache of the home-based businessperson, and the greatest opportunity to generate "unearned income" (a net gain in dollars at the end of the year resulting, in this case, from tax-favored arrangements, instead of actual business productivity). Now that you know the potential of the various tax topic areas, think of how you can honestly take advantage of them. Get professional help on actually implementing your ideas and keeping your applications of them current and legal over time—they change constantly, for better and for worse. If he or she is good, your tax adviser will more than pay for the fees in tax dollars and IRS penalties saved.

Chapter 14

Insuring the Home-Based Business*

No matter how limited the scope of your home-based business activities, there are implications for your present insurance coverage. The increased risks may be negligible, but still require you to at least acknowledge the existence of the business in your residence. Some kinds of home businesses pose substantial new risk exposures that require specialized coverage. This chapter reviews the basics of insuring a business and gives you a starting point for a meaningful exploration of your needs with a qualified professional.

HOME-BASED BUSINESS INSURANCE MINIMUMS

When you plan your home office, consider first how it will alter the pattern of activities that now constitute the lifecycle of your residence.

* The author acknowledges the contribution of the Education Department of the Insurance Information Institute in New York. Their *Risk Management and Business Insurance* (1988) publication constitutes the primary resource for the basic insurance aspects of the discussion that follows, unless otherwise noted. Illustrations and accompanying definitions are used with that organization's permission. Adaptation to the home-business environment was done by the author and is not meant to imply Insurance Information Institute endorsement. The Institute is an educational, fact-finding and communications organization supported by 300 insurance companies that provide property, liability, fidelity, surety, and marine coverages.

How will things be different when the family wakes up in the morning and begins another day? Will the cast of characters and what they do be significantly different? What will change in the flow of outsiders coming into the home? Will additional equipment pose new risks? Will the value of property in the home increase? What kinds of additional activities will be projected from the home and into the community—business use of the family car, and so on?

It is apparent that your homeowner's insurance package may need some augmentation. There are risks that are logical extensions of the kinds of things already covered by the basic homeowner's policy—property exposures like fire and theft, for example—liability exposures like an outsider falling down your front steps.

As a bare minimum, you must confer with your insurance agent and do what is necessary to:

- Be assured that the act of conducting business from the home does not nullify any of your existing coverage
- Identify any special endorsements or riders that might be added to extend prudent business coverage to the dual purpose residence and home business
- Explore what other coverages might be advisable, either now or as your business grows.

It is neither wise nor possible to cover every potential risk. To some extent, you will be "self-insuring" your home-based business—standing ready to absorb the loss personally in the unlikely event that it occurs.

A good broker or agent with experience in commercial insurance will be able to assist you in the essential task of identifying risks, exploring possible insurance solutions to the problems posed, and deciding on a balanced coverage that matches your risks. It is desirable to have a single broker do this since overlapping exposures can sometimes be compensated for in a balanced package.

A great deal of common sense should be apparent as you and your insurance adviser evaluate and resolve your needs. Every home-based business will have different requirements. Some will relate to the residence and exposures occurring there, others will involve professional activities during long distance telephone conversations that result in someone else's perceived loss—a highly paid executive loses his position because of a recruiter's lack of discretion, for example.

Begin with the basic coverage prudent for your particular circumstances, products, and activities. Use the next section to prepare yourself for the possibility of broader needs as your home-based business impacts on the lives and property of still more people.

INCREASING YOUR INSURANCE AWARENESS

As a home-based businessperson, you will not be having a full-time risk manager on staff. The task of identifying and managing risks that could pose threats to the continued operation of your business is one that you and your insurance broker will share. The illustrations and brief definitions provide a graphic overview of how insurance can help the businessperson deal with various kinds of risks.

Property Losses

In using your home and its contents in the conduct of your business, you face the possibility of losses associated with that property. Your unique situation requires you to have the dual business/residential roles of the property understood and covered by the insurance you determine to be necessary.

Physical Damage   Losses resulting from such physical phenomena as fires, storms, and vandalism are obvious risks and standard insurance products are available to cover them. Less obvious, but essential to your total assessment of risk, is the impact of such physical damage on your ability to do business—business shutdown, lawsuits by injured clients or employees, and even the lost services of one of the business' principals.

Loss of Property Use   You probably wouldn't think of the sanctions of a regulatory body as an insurable risk, but it might be. If you have a legitimately operating business in your home and you are forced to close by a change in the zoning laws, for example, the resulting business disruption might be insured. This is the kind of risk that would almost certainly be "self-insured" by the typical home-based businessperson. However, as the business grows and the potential loss from such a problem takes on real monetary importance, remember the point deserves discussion with your insurance adviser.

Criminal Activity Crime isn't likely to be high among your concerns as a low-profile home-based business. Theft of valuable business property such as computers or more specialized things unique to your profession does warrant attention. There are less direct risks under the criminal category that you must also remain alert to—white collar crime is a possibility, if you employ others and they are in a position to wrongfully remove value from your business. That might take the form of money directly or essential proprietary information. It is an area of risk that deserves your constant awareness as you trade in professional knowledge, products, and procedures.

Business Interruption Loss

Making your home a place of business doesn't alter the significance of being denied its use for generating income should a fire or other loss occur. You are out of business and will need additional resources to compensate for the revenues lost by the forced closing and pay the added expense of temporary space while your home-office is being replaced.

Less obvious, but an equally important source of business interruption for the home-based entrepreneur, is a nonphysical loss that denies an important source of income. It might happen as the result of a fire or natural disaster effecting a major firm to whom you supply products or services as a subcontractor. As a small businessperson, you are perhaps more vulnerable to the loss of a single source than your larger competitors. Keep the possibility in mind as the potential damage from such an eventuality grows significant for your home-based business.

Liability Loss

You will want to cover your residence and the business-related exposures for claims of potential liability. You and your company may be held responsible for damages or personal injuries. They might result from court determined negligence, statutory obligations such as workers' compensation laws, or contract provisions for which you are held accountable.

Liability to the Public If you or someone who works for your home-based business do something—or fail to so something—that results in loss or injury to a member of the public, you may face a lawsuit to recover the damages and, perhaps, inflict a punishment. The loss can escalate even further and generalize to the community if you cause a forest fire or violate a statute in place for the public good.

Liability to Employees If you have others working for you and they are injured in the course of their duties, you may be held responsible. In most states, a minimum level of coverage for this class of injury is mandated by workers' compensation laws. The wisdom of additional coverage, if any, is something to be resolved with the advise of an insurance professional.

Key Person Losses

In the home-based business, you *are* the key person. The concept is the same whether you are a one-person operation or others share important roles. Insurance is used as a way to ease the shock to the business if such a crucial human asset is lost—an irreplaceable employee talent or a financially critical owner.

Key Employees Whether the worker in question is you or someone you hire, key employee insurance provides the resources to buffer the company against lost productivity, recruit, hire, and train a replacement.

Key Owners In the case of a lost owner, the very continuation of the business is at stake. Insurance can make it possible for it to pass to new owners or a restructured partnership or corporation. In the small, home-based business, the problems of owner disability or death are critical. Business continuation insurance may be warranted when you have a firm with value that might ·be passed to others if you are no longer able to be the principal. For many one-person small businesses, there is insufficient residual value outside the principal to provide a

basis for such continuation. As discussed in Chapter 11, the sole proprietor's business dies with him. Business continuation insurance may
have a place in your planning if you have adopted the partnership or
corporate form of organization.

Loss Control

In your home-based business you have a large measure of control over
the potential losses faced by your firm.

Avoiding Loss Exposures   One of your continuing actions as a small
business owner is the appraisal of risks. When you sense that you are
engaged in an activity that brings with it an unreasonable chance that
you will have your business disrupted or sued, a change of practices is
warranted. An executive recruiting firm may find that it is more prudent to remain small and operate with a cadre of experienced professionals than to increase the likelihood of suits brought on by the
actions of an inexperienced and under-supervised expansion staff.

Minimizing Losses   Losses in some phases of business activity will
occur in spite of your best management practices. When that happens, your goal becomes one of limiting the scope of your anticipated
losses. Order frequently in small quantities instead of maintaining a
large inventory, for example. Use alarms and other devices to detect
fires and break ins before extensive loss occurs.

Risk Retention

The term self-insurance was used earlier in this chapter to describe
risks that owners choose to retain. It can be as simple as being ignorant
of the risk and inadvertently carrying the potential for loss. Or it can
be a calculated risk retention like the very specific ones associated with
deductibles where the first increment of loss is met by the owner instead of the insurer. Risk retention is a matter of business judgment
that you will have to make as a home-based company with a great deal
of ability to control your exposures by steering clear of imprudent risk
situations.

Risk Transfer

Another way to deal with business risks is to transfer them to an insurance company or someone else who might bear them for you.

Non-Insurance Risk Transfer   The home-based business will rely heavily on this form of protection. It is accomplished by identifying activities that are necessary in your business but that can be done by an outside firm. If you need to have deliveries made, assign the task to a company that can do it on a fee basis and free you of the burden of operating a business within your business. If the delivery person damages someone's property, it isn't your problem and the owner of the delivery business must be prepared to carry the risk you have transferred to him by the consignment of the delivery. Other examples include using storage facilities rather than bearing the cost of insuring the safety of materials kept at home, or the practice of not ordering inventory until it is needed. Drop shipping, in the case of a home-based mail order business would be the ultimate case of transferring both inventory and delivery risks to another firm.

Insurance Risk Transfer   The most prevalent form of risk transfer is to an insurance company. These firms exist for the purpose of pooling risks and distributing the cost across a large number of clients. When one suffers a loss, the insurance company pays using the proceeds from the payments made by the larger group. The advantages of insurance as the device for transferring risk include guaranteed protection against large losses for relatively small and predictable payments. Insurance provides the kind of certainty against loss that lenders, suppliers, and other businesses expect of you.

Using Business Insurance

The Insurance Information Institute (*Risk Management and Business Insurance*, 1988) concludes its recommendations to potential small business owners with advice to see the similarities, but make the necessary distinctions, between personal and business insurance. As a home-based businessperson, this is all the more necessary since the two are so intertwined.

Package Insurance Policies Your home is already covered by a homeowners policy that packages liability and property insurance common to the vast majority of residential situations. The same approach is taken in the business side of the industry where the all embracing package is known generically as the Commercial Package Policy or the CPP. Chances are your home-based business will be insured by some combination of these two standards of the insurance business. They will be matched and examined for both overlapping coverages and holes that must be plugged by specific additions unique to your particular business activity.

Business Applications of Life Insurance Key person insurance was mentioned earlier. A major role of life insurance in business is to provide the surviving partners, shareholders, or family members with the money necessary to purchase the deceased principal's share and ease the continuation process.

Insurance Services

Large insurance firms are complex organizations that provide more than the loss coverages discussed in the preceding sections.

They are also staffed with professionals whose job it is to preempt loss through advising policyholders on how to avoid problems. When the claims do materialize, the expert legal defense provided by your insurance carrier will be as essential to your survival as their ability to pay any resulting judgment.

The return to useful employment for you or an injured employee may be aided by the extensive rehabilitation services maintained by those segments of the insurance industry that deal with worker's compensation.

The Insurance Marketplace

You would be well-advised to seek the guidance of your agent or broker early in the process of establishing your business. A logical first point of contact is your present homeowner's policy carrier. Find out if the same firm also deals in the insurance needs of small business owners. It may be that you will be referred to another agent within the same firm whose expertise is in the commercial lines you now need to address.

Free advice of professional caliber is something that you won't see a lot of in the development of your home-based business. Insurance can be the exception if you can locate a qualified agent who sees the promise of expanding future business from your fledgling enterprise. If you haven't had the experience recently, you will be favorably impressed with the growing professionalism of the insurance industry. That is doubly true in the commercial lines where the representatives are highly trained specialists who can do a lot for you in defining a reasonable array of coverages, limits, and deductibles to meet your needs.

POLICIES TO CONSIDER

Home-based businesses vary widely in their characteristics, needs, and risk exposures. Some of the services listed here may extend beyond the purview of the small start up, but they may be just the thing for the entrepreneur whose home-based business is suddenly funding a very full level business activity. Keep these possibilities in mind as your home enterprise grows. This section has been adapted from the "Owning A Business" chapter of *Your Guide to USAA Services,* 1989 Edition (pp. 31–34).

- *Business packages* that include a full range of commercial insurance coverages, both property and liability. Included might be such things as commercial auto, commercial umbrella, and worker's compensation.

- *Aviation insurance* may be a necessity. It doesn't take a private Lear jet to expose your business to risk in the aviation area if a private plane is used for business purposes. Be sure you are covered if you are a private pilot and your home-based business tempts you to enjoy its convenience in support of your commercial activities.

- *Health insurance* for a home-based business. Depending on your situation, it may be possible to arrange for tax-favored sick pay plans that provide continuation of salary payments to disabled employees while allowing an IRS deduction for the premium.

- *Split-dollar insurance* is a possible way to have your business pay for personal life insurance.

- *Salary continuation/differed compensation* is a method of compensating executives and highly paid employees on an individual basis at the sole discretion of the employer. Acts as an excellent supplement to an employer-sponsored pension or profit-sharing plan.

- *Key person insurance* protects your business against financial loss caused by the death, disability, or termination of employment of a vital member of your firm.

- *Buy-sell agreement* protects and insures the orderly transfer of the ownership of a business interest if one partner or stockholder dies, retires, becomes disabled, or dissolves the partnership. Both Key Person Insurance and funded Buy-Sell Agreement Insurance offer tax-deferred cash build-up that can be used to supplement your company's retirement plan, or to fund acquisitions.

- *Universal life insurance,* properly planned, surplus earnings can accumulate through the cash value of a life insurance policy without the cash value being considered as "retained earnings," thus avoiding a possible tax. Life insurance can also provide collateral for a business loan.

- *Pension plan funding*—mutual funds and annuities—can be used to fund your profit-sharing plan, SEP/IRA, or funding-only pension plan.

Note that your form of business organization is a factor in the kinds of policies that will be useful in your situation. Refer to Chapter 11 and Chapter 13 for further information to help guide your decisions.

OTHER INSURANCE NEEDS

Along with considerations of business and homeowners coverages, don't ignore the needs of your family and employees for such things as major medical insurance, disability insurance, and life insurance. Have another look at the ramifications of your form of business organization in Chapter 11 to determine the company's ability to pay for all or part of such coverages as a business expense.

Professional associations are a worthy source of group insurance information. Consider what is available from these sources and use them for comparison shopping with what is being offered by your local agent. Don't overlook the possible value of the personal service provided by the local insurance professional, but politely challenge them to meet the competition of your professional group policy offerings.

Liability insurance for various professional groups can be extremely specialized and expensive. Again, comparison shopping is advised and do not overlook the mass purchasing power of your societies and associations.

LIABILITY INSURANCE—SOME SPECIAL NOTES*

The same phenomenon that has closed municipal playgrounds and driven thousands of gynecologists out of the practice of delivering babies has real ramifications for the home-based business. This discussion is directed specifically to the personnel placement business, but the examples will increase your sensitivity to the kinds of exposures you might face regardless of your home-based specialty.

Scope of the Problem

The five-year periods 1975 to 1980 and 1981 to 1986 reflected the following changes in the claims activity related to one agency's personnel consultant and temporary help services clients:

- The number of claims filed rose 64 percent.
- The total amount of these claims skyrocketed 421 percent.
- The dollar amount of legal fees paid to litigate these claims shot up 316 percent.
- Payments in settlement of these claims leaped by 107 percent.
- Total claim costs rose by 114 percent.

Home-based professionals in many service categories face similar trends in their vulnerability to costly litigation.

---

* An industry leader in the personnel services industry, World Wide Facilities, Inc. of Garden City, New York (Lesberg, 1987), is the source for the following information.

Questions and Answers about Liability Insurance

Several concerns are of interest to any home-based service business person. The two basic types of coverage you will likely encounter are errors and omissions and bonding. The questions and answers will help you develop a sensitivity for the relationship between you and the firm that writes your coverage—and shows what can go wrong if you fail to communicate precisely.

Q: Why do I need both an E&O policy and a bond? Isn't one enough?

A: The Errors & Omissions policy covers wrongful acts such as negligence, errors, misstatements, omissions, and slander. It specifically excludes criminal, dishonest, and/or fraudulent acts, which are the activities covered by the bond. The combination of the E&O policy and the bond gives you the protection you and your firm must have.

Q: Who is covered under my professional liability policy? Are secretaries covered, and if not, should they be?

A: The policy is designed to cover your officers, partners, counselors, and all employees listed on your application. We recommend that all member of your staff who come in contact with clients and/or applicants be covered, including secretaries. This is to protect you should they improperly release resumes or other information.

Q: Why do I have to fill out a lengthy renewal application again? Can't you just use the information that you have on file from last year?

A: No. Updated information is necessary. Your application asks very specific questions about your business and the types of services provided to enable us to ascertain your coverage needs. Your industry is changing rapidly and you may be entering a new business area excluded from coverage under your policy. Or perhaps a special endorsement is necessary to protect certain exposures. Should a loss occur in a service not shown on your application, coverage may be denied on the basis that a material misrepresentation has been made.

Let's say you place a licensed stockbroker whose error results in a loss to your client, and a claim is made. The insurer will likely examine the application to see if this specific placement service is shown. If is is, and no exclusions show, the insurer has to respond to the claim. Otherwise, coverage could be denied. You avoid this possibility by completing your application and returning it as soon as possible. (Lesberg, undated, p. 4)

Eileen Lesberg cites some examples of how a service business can find itself facing a liability claim. While these have been abstracted from her personnel industry newsletter, the parallels for any service business—including those run from a home office are apparent.

A personnel consulting firm sent an applicant's resume to a subsidiary company. The resume was circulated through the company and wound up in the personnel department of the home office. The applicant was fired. He sued and collected $10,000 in damages. This is just one of 47 cases in which World Wide Customers have made the mistake of sending a applicants resume to a current employer.

An employment agency sued a former employee, claiming ownership of the files the counselor had taken with him. A countersuit resulted in the counselor being awarded $16,000; legal fees amounted to $30,000.

Sued for making slanderous remarks about a former employee, an employment agency was ordered to pay $15,000. Legal expenses were also $15,000.

A lawsuit involving medical costs was brought against a counselor who erred in interpreting health coverages. He had incorrectly advised that medical insurance would pay for a home health aide obtainable through a temporary help service firm. Legal expenses exceeded $50,000.

An applicant was placed by a personnel consulting firm after a check of just one reference—the applicant's wife, who gave a glowing recommendation. After losing contracts, the personnel firm's client discovered that the applicant had neither the college degree nor the experience claimed. A lawsuit against the consulting firm seeks more than $250,000 in damages.

Because a temporary help firm's employee delayed in submitting the necessary laboratory information, an applicant for an insurance policy died before the policy could be insured. Legal action charging the consultant with negligence resulted in a judgment of $155,000, exclusive of legal fees. (Lesberg, undated, pp. 2–3)

While it isn't news that we live in a highly litigious society, it may be an eye-opener for the prospective home-based business person to review these examples and see how the same kinds of actions could be brought against their low profile enterprises. The threat of liability exposures such as these should not be any reason to avoid establishing your business, but it should be a part of your thinking as you choose your insurance and legal form of organization.

CONCLUSION

There is no need to overemphasize insurance for the home-based business, but being naive about it can lead to tragic results in the event of an improperly covered loss. With the perspectives gained in this chapter, you are in a position to note what appear to be the likely risks your business will face. Talk it over with a competent insurance professional and see what kinds of packages might meet your specific needs (and how they should be modified). Many of the extras cost very little, it is just a matter of being sufficiently aware to ask. Liability insurance is tremendously important for a practicing professional and it is highly individualized by specialty—be sure you have sufficient coverage to at least present a strong defense if you are unfortunate enough to need it. Don't overlook the positive side of the insurance business as it relates to your self-employed status. Many of the products in these lines are of investment quality and come with special tax advantages as well.

Chapter 15

Success, Failure, and Finding Help

Home-based businesses require sensitive management. The problems posed in succeeding and failing businesses are different, but the challenges are often of similar magnitude for a sputtering failure or a runaway success. Both call for decisions that will test your ability to locate and direct the prudent use of precious resources—time, money, and other people's expertise.

PROBLEMS YOU'D LIKE TO HAVE (MAYBE)

There are few things more gratifying than to have your business prove itself in the marketplace. Demand for your product or service is a high form of personal and professional compliment. However, you must be prepared to cope with the problems of success. This can be doubly true for the home-based business whose very growth can threaten its character and attractiveness—to you, your clients, and the neighbors who may be less than forgiving of the increased activity.

For the true home-based businessperson who wants to remain in the valued sanctuary that they have created outside the organizational world, success can be bittersweet. It is possible to keep the home office as the center for an ever larger enterprise, but it calls for deliberate effort. The temptation to go traditional can be attractive and it warrants careful consideration.

The decision on how to handle burgeoning success in your special environment is closely linked to the reasons that brought you to this unique style of business in the first place. For some it was a necessity that required the economies of living and working at home to make the start-up possible. Others began from the home base because it offered the anonymity required to start the business while maintaining a full-time position in the traditional world. Still another group craved the mildly anti-establishment lifestyle that gave them a continuing and profitable place in their profession, but freed them of the down side irritants—commuting, wearing of the uniform on a daily basis, the corporate pecking order, and operating formalities they longed to leave behind.

Success at home will be handled differently by different people. Those who used the home office as a necessary stepping stone will take the groundwork laid there and move on to head their own traditional enterprise. The establishment leavers will seek a way to enjoy their success without reverting to the organizational limitations they do not want—someone else's, or their own.

For those now ready for traditional growth, the path will be the smoother for having proven their concept in the low-risk environment of the home-based business. By the time the road is clear to hanging out a shingle in the commercial zone, there should be a history of successfully operating as a business. Capital raising should come more readily now that there is an established banking relationship and small business loans that have been repaid on schedule. Best of all there are established accounts and income tax forms to add credence to the fact that you are at the helm of a reliably productive enterprise. You have a track record that says to your potential creditors "there is a plausible pattern of cash flow—this business has demonstrated an ability to meet its obligations."

For either the "going traditional" or "staying at home" success story, there are refinements in the operation that should be considered. If the organizational form assumed at the outset was a simple one, you should examine with your attorney and accountant the wisdom of forming an S corporation, or whatever would be most advantageous. One of the nice problems of a comfortably prospering independent business, even if it remains a sideline to your full-time professional position, is how to legally and ethically optimize the extraction of value from the business. The overriding consideration is taxation and how to delay or avoid it. Your profitable home-based business opens doors to financial planning options that do not exist for those who merely draw a paycheck—even if you still draw a paycheck.

SUCCESS AND FAILURE (ITS RELATIVE)

A well-conceived home business can provide you with a relatively safe testing ground for your concept. It will also measure your suitability as an independent businessperson. These prerequisites need re-examination after a period time. The attractiveness of the home-based start up is the limited down side risk—to both your balance sheet and your ego. If you find your enterprise fails the crucial tests of financial viability and personal satisfaction, take another look and decide whether you want to make the necessary adjustments or acknowledge a lesson learned about your likes and dislikes.

If the only problem is financial, you can get help in altering the way you do business or selecting another product or service. Satisfaction correlates closely with financial success and the cure for that ailment may follow the improved prospects for your bottom line.

Finding that the relatively lonely workstyle of the home office doesn't suit your nature or inspire your best productivity can be another outcome. The solution might be taking your business into a more traditional setting, bringing in a partner or employee, or, if your heart is not in the business, taking yourself back into the organizational world the wiser for your experience.

Failure is too harsh a word for what is more apt to be a change of course for the home-based entrepreneur. Objective evaluation will leave options that include altering aspects of your operation and proceeding to what you have defined as success. Your challenge is to define a course that leaves you with an acceptable balance of lifestyle and business necessity.

If you conclude that operating a home-based business is not for you, count yourself fortunate in that you have taken the opportunity to look yourself in the eye and answer a question that many never resolve. The dream of being their own boss or achieving independence by an exercise of their own talents remains an unresolved possibility for most. It is a wonderful thing for many—a bona fide disappointment for others. Regardless of your end result, at least you know the

Figure 15–1 Success and failure: The buck stops with you in the home-based business.

answer to a question few will honestly explore. Whether the outcome is the inner contentment of increased self-knowledge or the rewards of unfettered commitment to your traditional career, your time as a home-based business person ,should pay rich dividends. Figure 15–1 suggests that you sit back and ponder how you could handle these relative outcomes—because in the home-based business, it will all depend on you.

SOURCES OF ADDITIONAL HELP AND INFORMATION

While advice is only of value when acted upon, informed decisions begin with respect for the experience of others who have tried what you are now attempting. Everyone comes to the task with different levels of experience and business skills. Select from the sources that follow to help fill the voids in your own repertoire. In addition to the items that follow:

- Scan the bibliography for publications not duplicated here.
- Check an 800 number directory for listings that relate to your interests.

- Visit the news stand for current periodicals that address your needs.
- Go to a good library and check the business reference section for directories and publications that can lead you to the information you seek.

Federal Government

Congressional Assistance—your Representative or Senator's office can be helpful in locating information and solving problems with government agencies. Call the capitol switchboard at 202-224-3121, or check with their office in your area.

Department of Commerce, 14th Street NW, Washington, DC 202-377-2000. (Second only to the SBA as a government source of information for business, first check for a local office near you—or call and ask for the location nearest you.)

Internal Revenue Service booklets:
  Business Use of Your Home, Publication 587
  Employer's Tax Guide, Circular E
  Information on Excise Taxes, Publication 505
  Self-Employment Tax, Publication 533
  Tax Guide for Small Business, Publication 334
  Tax Information on Depreciation, Publication 534
  Tax Information on Retirement Plans for the Self-Employed, Publication 560
  Your Federal Income Tax, Publication 17

Start-up forms that you may need from the IRS include:
  Application for Employer Identification Number (Form SS-4)
  Employee's Withholding Allowance Certificate (Form W-4)
  Employer's Annual Unemployment Tax Return (Form 940)
  Employer's Quarterly Federal Tax Return (Form 941)
  Employer's Wage and Tax Statement (Form W-2)

Reconciliation/Transmittal of Income and Tax Statement (Form W-3)

Check your local telephone book for the IRS telephone number for your region or call 800-424-1040 (202-488-3100).

Small Business Administration (SBA), 1441 L Street, NW, Washington, DC 20416 800-368-5855/202-653-7561. Call the Small Business Answer Desk to learn who can best assist you with your question.

State Government—most states have a central point of contact to assist people who are trying to develop businesses in their state. Call and ask for a referral for your particular concern. Use this contact as your starting point in your search for the information needed to help you make your business grow. They can be helpful in guiding you to local federal and private sources of information and assistance as well as state programs. The following list was adapted from *The Small Business Resource Guide* (1988, pp. 27–56):

Alabama Development Office, State Capitol, Montgomery, AL 36130 205-263-0048 or in state: 800-248-0033.

Alaska Division of Business Development, Department of Commerce & Economic Development, P. O. Box D, Juneau, AK 99811 907-465-2017.

Arizona Office of Community Finance, Department of Commerce, 1700 West Washington Street, 4th Floor, Phoenix, AZ 85007 602-255-5705.

Arkansas Small Business Information Center, Industrial Development Commission, 1 State Capitol Mall, Room 4C-300, Little Rock, AR 501-682-3358.

California Office of Small Business, Department of Commerce, 1121 L Street, Suite 600, Sacramento, CA 95814 916-445-6545.

Colorado Business Information Center, Office of Regulatory Reform, 1525 Sherman Street, Room 110, Denver, CO 80203 303-866-3933.

Connecticut Small Business Services, Department of Economic Development, 210 Washington Street, Hartford, CT 06106 203-566-4051.

Delaware Development Office, 99 King's Highway, P. O. Box 1401, Dover, DE 19903 302-736-4271.

District of Columbia Office of Business and Economic Development, 7th Floor, 1111 E Street, NW, Washington DC 20004 202-727-6600.

Florida Bureau of Business Assistance, Department of Commerce, 107 W. Gaines Street, Tallahassee, FL 32339-2000 904-488-9357; in state: 800-343-0771.

Georgia Department of Industry and Trade, 230 Peachtree Road, NW, Atlanta, GA 30303 404-656-3584.

Hawaii Small Business Information Service, 250 South King Street, Room 724, Honolulu, HI 96813 808-548-7645.

Idaho Economic Development Division, Department of Commerce, State Capitol, Room 108, Boise, ID 83720 208-334-3416.

Illinois Small Business Assistance Bureau, Department of Commerce and Community Affairs, 620 E. Adams Street, Springfield, IL 62701 217-785-6282; in state: 800-252-2923.

Indiana Division of Business Expansion, Department of Commerce, One North Capital, Suite 700, Indianapolis, IN 46204-2288 317-232-3527; in state: 800-824-2476.

Iowa Bureau of Business/Targeted Small Business Development, Department of Economic Development, 200 E. Grand Avenue, Des Moines, IA 50309 515-281-8310; in state: 800-532-1216.

Kansas Division of Existing Industry Development, 400 SW Eighth Street, Fifth Floor, Topeka, KS 66603 913-296-5298.

Kentucky Small Business Division, Commerce Cabinet, Capitol Plaza Tower, 22nd Floor, Frankfort, KY 40601 502-564-4252; in state: 800-626-2250.

Louisiana Development Division, Office of Commerce and Industry, P. O. Box 94185, Baton Rouge, LA 70804-9185 504-342-5365.

Maine Business Development Division, State Development Office, State House, Augusta, ME 04333 207-872-3838; in state: 800-289-2659.

Maryland Office of Business and Industrial Development, Department of Economic and Employment Development, 45 Calvert Street, Annapolis, MD 21401 301-974-2946; in state: 800-654-7336.

Massachusetts Small Business Assistance Division, Department of Commerce, 100 Cambridge Street, 13th Floor, Boston, MA 02202 617-727-4295.

Michigan Business Ombudsman, Department of Commerce, P. O. Box 30107, Lansing, MI 48909 517-373-6242; in state: 800-232-2727.

Minnesota Small Business Assistance Office, Department of Trade and Economic Development, 900 American Center, 150 E. Kellogg Blvd., St. Paul, MN 55101 612-296-3871; in state: 800-652-9747.

Mississippi Small Business Bureau, Research and Development Center, 3825 Ridgewood Road, Jackson, MS 39211-6453 601-982-6231.

Missouri Small Business Development Office, Department of Economic Development, P. O. Box 118, Jefferson City, MO 65102 314-751-4982 or -8411.

Montana Business Assistance Division, Department of Commerce, 1424 Ninth Avenue, Helena, MT 59620·406-444-3923; in state: 800-221-8015.

Nebraska Small Business Division, Department of Economic Development, P. O. Box 94666, 301 Centennial Mall South, Lincoln, NE 68509 402-471-4167.

Nevada Office of Community Services, 1100 East William, Suite 116, Carson City, NV 89710 702-885-4602.

New Hampshire Office of Industrial Development, 105 Loudon Road, Prescott Park, Bldg. 2, Concord, NH 03301 603-271-2591

New Jersey Office of Small Business Assistance, Department of Commerce and Economic Development, 1 West State Street, CN 835, Trenton, NJ 08625 609-984-4442.

New Mexico Economic Development Division, Department of Economic Development and Tourism, 1100 St. Francis Drive, Santa Fe, NM 87503 505-827-0300; in state: 800-545-2040.

New York Division of Small Business, Department of Economic Development, 230 Park Avenue, Room 834, New York, NY 10169 212-309-0400.

North Carolina Small Business Development Division, Department of Commerce, Dobbs Building, Room 2019, 430 N. Salisbury Street, Raleigh, NC 27611 919-733-7978.

North Dakota Small Business Coordinator, Economic Development Commission, Liberty Memorial Building, Bismark, ND 58505 701-224-2810; in state: 800-472-2100.

Ohio Small & Developing Business Division, Ohio Department of Development, P. O. Box 1001, Columbus, OH 43266-0101 614-466-1876; in state 800-282-1085.

Oklahoma Department of Commerce, 6601 Broadway extension, Oklahoma City, OK 73116 405-521-2401.

Oregon Economic Development Department, 595 Cottage Street, NE, Salem, OR 97310 503-373-1200, 800-547-7842; in state: 800-233-3306.

Pennsylvania Small Business Action Center, Department of Commerce, 404 Forum Building, Harrisburg, PA 17120 717-783-5700.

Puerto Rico Commonwealth, Department of Commerce, Box S, 4275 Old San Juan Station, San Juan, PR 00905 809-758-4747.

Rhode Island Small Business Development Division, Department of Economic Development, 7 Jackson Walkway, Providence, RI 02903 401-277-2601.

South Carolina Business Development and Assistance Division, State Development Board, P. O. Box 927, Columbia, SC 29202 803-737-0400; in state: 800-922-6684.

South Dakota Governor's Office of Economic Development, Capital Lake Plaza, Pierre, SD 57501 605-773-5032; in state: 800-952-3625.

Tennessee Small Business Office, Department of Economic and Community Development, 320 6th Avenue, North, 7th Floor, Rachel Jackson Building, Nashville, TN 37219 615-741; in state: 800-872-7201.

Texas Small Business Division, Department of Commerce Economic Development Commission, P. O. Box 12728, Capitol Station, 410 East Fifth Street, Austin, TX 78711 512-472-5059.

Utah Small Business Development Center, 660 South Second Street, #418, Salt Lake City, UT 84111 801-581-7905.

Vermont Agency of Development and Community Affairs, The Pavilion, 109 State Street, Montpelier, VT 05602 802-828-3221; in state: 800-622-4553.

Virginia Small Business & Financial Services, Department of Economic Development, 1000 Washington Building, Richmond, VA 23219 804-786-3791.

Washington Small Business Development Center, 441 Todd Hall, Washington State University, Pullman, WA 99164 509-335-1576.

West Virginia Small Business Development Center Division, Governor's Office of Community and Industrial Development, Capitol Complex, Charleston, WV 25305 304-348-2960.

Wisconsin Small Business Ombudsman, Department of Development, 123 W. Washington Avenue, P. O. Box 7970, Madison, WI 53707 608-266-0562; in state: 800-435-7287.

Wyoming Economic Development and Stabilization Board, Herschler Building, 3rd Floor East, Cheyenne, WY 82002 307-777-7287.

Private Publications

Bly, Robert W. & Gary Blake. *Out on Your Own: From Corporate to Self-Employment.* New York: John Wiley & Sons.

Cohen, William A. *Building a Mail Order Business.* New York: John Wiley & Sons.

Cohen, William A. *The Entrepreneur & Small Business Financial Problem Solver.* New York: John Wiley & Sons.

Connor, Jr., Richard A. & Jeffrey P. Davidson. *Marketing Your Consulting and Professional Services.* New York: John Wiley & Sons.

Davidson, Jeffrey P. *The Marketing Sourcebook for Small Business.* New York: John Wiley & Sons.

Diamond, Michael R. and Julie L. Williams. *How to Incorporate: A Handbook For Entrepreneurs and Professionals.* New York: John Wiley & Sons.

Dougherty, David. *From Technical Professional to Entrepreneur.* New York: John Wiley & Sons.

Eyler, David R. *The Executive Moonlighter.* New York: John Wiley & Sons. A how-to-do-it on keeping your job while developing a professional business after hours. Chapters on executive recruiting, consulting, seminar and trade show promotion, professional speaking, money brokering, and computer related services.

Goldstein, Arnold S. *Starting Your Subchapter "S" Corporation: How to Build a Business the Right Way.* New York: John Wiley & Sons.

Gosden, Freeman F. *Direct Marketing Success.* New York: John Wiley & Sons.

Holtz, Herman. *Choosing and Using a Consultant.* New York: John Wiley & Sons.

Holtz, Herman. *How to Make Money with Your Desktop Computer.* New York: John Wiley & Sons.

Holtz, Herman. *How to Succeed as an Independent Consultant.* 2nd edition. New York: John Wiley & Sons, 1988. (Also on tape)

Home BusinessLine. American Home Business Association, 397 Post Road, Darien, CT 06820 800-433-6361/203-655-4380.

Home Offices & Workspaces, the Editors of Sunset Books and Sunset Magazine. 1986, 96 pages. Sunset-Lane Publishing Company, 80 Willow Road, Menlo Park, CA 94025-3691, 800-227-7346 or 415-321-3600. LC 86-80869; ISBN 0-376-01303-6.

J. K. Lasser's Your Income Tax, 1989, J. K. Lasser Institute,1989, 501 pages. Simon & Schuster Reference Division, 200 Old Tappan Road, Old Tappan, NJ 07675, 212-373-7700.

Jordan, Joanna. *How to Get Rich Sooner Than You Think, Volumes 1 & 2.* Sterling, VA: New Start Publications, Inc., 1987, 108/122 pages. (This is a paperback set of books promoted in the get-rich-quick fashion, but worthy of the modest price of less than $15. It gives you a good overview of mail order marketing, sources for acquiring services, including an interesting list of private label suppliers.)

Kaye, Harvey. *Inside the Technical Consulting Business:Launching and Building Your Independent Practice.* New York: John Wiley & Sons.

Lindsey, Jennifer. *Start-up Money: Raise What You Need for Your Small Business.* New York: John Wiley & Sons.

Lumley, James E. A. *Sell It By Mail.* New York: John Wiley & Sons.

Lynn, Gary S. *From Concept to Market.* New York: John Wiley & Sons.

MANA Research Bulletins, Laguna Hills, CA: Manufacturers' Agents National Association 714-859-4040.

National Home Business Report. P. O. Box 2137, Naperville, IL 60566.

O'Hara, Patrick D. *SBA Loans.* New York: John Wiley & Sons.

Porterfield, James D. *Selling on the Phone.* New York: John Wiley & Sons. (Also on tape)

Risk Management and Business Insurance. New York: Insurance Information Institute, 1988, 13 pages.

Risk Management: A Small Business Primer. Washington: U. S. Chamber of Commerce, 1987, 78 pages.

Slutsky, Jeff. *Street Smart Marketing.* New York: John Wiley & Sons.

Small Business Reports, Small Business Reporter, Bank of America, Department 3401, P. O. Box 37000, San Francisco, CA 94137.

Telecommunications Ideas to Grow On: A Planning Tool for Small Business Growth. Basking Ridge, NJ: AT&T, 1986. 800-533-9782 Ext. 6101 (1989 revision pending).

Telecommuting Report. Electronic Services Unlimited, 79 Fifth Avenue, New York, NY 10003.

Telecommuting Review: The Gordon Report. Telespan Publishing, 50 West Palm Street, CA 91001.

The Light Book: A Guide for Lighting Your Home. Cleveland, OH: General Electric, 1988, 36 pages 800-626-2000.

The Small Business Resource Guide. Washington: Braddock Communications, Inc., 1988, 135 pages. (An SBA & AT&T initiative, 202-463-5503).

Working at Home. The Editors of Better Homes and Gardens. 1985, 160 pages. Meredith Corporation, 1716 Locust Street, Des Moines, IA 50336, 515-284-3000. (No longer in print as of this writing). LC 84-61313; ISBN 0-696-02173-0.

Private Groups

American Home Business Association, 397 Post Road, Darien, CT 06820 203-655-4380 800-433-6361. (Newsletter, hot line advisory service, group insurance plans, buying service, discounts, etc.)

Entrepreneur, 2392 Morse Avenue, Irvine, CA 92714 800-421-2300; in state: 800-352-7449. Helpful, practical, how-to-do-it business handbooks on over 200 specific businesses.

National Association of Women Business Owners (NAWBO), 600 South Federal Street, Suite 400, Chicago, IL 60605 312-922-0465.

National Small Business United (NSBU), 1155 15th Street, NW, Suite 710, Washington, DC 20005 202-293-8830.

RSE Marketing, Route 1, Box 435, Weyers Cave, VA 24486. You will receive a small collection of checklists and worksheets for developing practical estimates of your cash flow and tax obligations. $10.00.

The Chamber of Commerce of the U. S., 1615 H. Street, NW, Washington, DC 20062 202-659-6000. (Also check your local and state chambers of commerce.)

The National Federation of Independent Business (NFIB), 600 Maryland Avenue, SW, Suite 700, Washington, DC 20024 202-463-9000.

Appendix: Home-Based Business Tax Terms[1]

This appendix is abstracted from pages 474–478 of the book, *J. K. Lasser's Your Income Tax 1989*, prepared by J. K. Lasser Institute, © 1988. Used by permission of the publisher, J. K. Lasser Institute, New York, NY. Only selected terms judged to be of primary interest to home-based business owners were reproduced in this appendix.

Accrual method of accounting: A business method of accounting requiring income to be reported when earned and expenses to be deducted when incurred. However, deductions generally may not be claimed until economic performance has occurred.

Amortize: Writing off an investment in intangible assets over the projected life of the assets.

Asset: Anything owned that has cash or exchange value.

Audit: An IRS examination of your tax return, generally limited to a three-year period after you file.

[1]Adapted from the book, *J. K. Lasser's Your Income Tax 1989*, prepared by J. K. Lasser Institute, 1988. Used by permission of the publisher, J. K. Lasser Institute, New York, NY. This Appendix contains individual entries reproduced selectively from Lasser's Glossary/Treasury of Tax Terms, pages 474–478.

Away from home: A tax requirement for deducting travel expenses on a business trip. Sleeping arrangements are required for at least one night before returning home.

Basis: Generally, the amount paid for property. You need to know your "basis" to figure gain or loss on a sale.

Calendar year: A year that ends on December 31.

Capital: The excess of assets over liabilities.

Capital asset: Property subject to capital gain or loss treatment. Almost all assets ;you own are considered capital assets, except for certain business assets or works you created.

Capital expenses: Costs that are not currently deductible and that are added to the basis of property. A capital expense generally increases the value of property. When added to depreciable property, the cost is deductible over the life of the asset.

Capital gain or loss: The difference between amount realized and adjusted basis on the sale or exchange of capital assets. Capital gain is taxed the same as other types of income, even if it is long-term. Capital losses are deducted first against capital gains, and then against up to $3,000 of other income.

Capital loss carryover: A capital loss that is not deductible because it exceed the annual $3,000 capital loss ceiling. A carryover loss may be deducted from capital gains of later years plus up to $3,000 of ordinary income.

Capitalization: Adding a cost or expense to the basis of the property.

Carry back: A tax technique for receiving a refund of back taxes by applying a deduction or credit from a current tax year to a prior tax year. For example, a business net operating loss may be carried back for three years.

Carry forward: A tax technique of applying a loss or credit from a current year to a later year. For example, a business net operating loss may be carried forward 15 years instead of being carried back for three years.

Cash method of accounting: Reporting income when actually or constructively received and deducting expenses when paid. Certain businesses may not use the cash method.

Casualty loss: Loss from an unforeseen and sudden event that is deductible, subject to a 10% income floor for personal losses.

Deductions: Items directly reducing income. Personal deductions such as for mortgage interest, state and local taxes and charitable contributions are allowed only if deductions are itemized on Schedule A, but certain deductions, such as for alimony, capital losses, business losses, IRA and Keogh deductions are deducted from gross income even if itemized deductions are not claimed.

Deferred compensation: A portion of earnings withheld by an employer or put into a retirement plan for distribution to the employee at a later date. If certain legal requirements are met, the deferred amount is not taxable until actually paid, for example, after retirement.

Depreciable property: A business or income-producing asset with a useful life exceeding one year.

Depreciation: Writing off the cost of depreciable property over a period of years, usually its class life or recovery period specified in the tax law.

Depreciation recapture: An amount of gain on the sale of certain depreciable property that is treated as ordinary income, rather than capital gain. Recapture is computed on Form 4797.

Dividend: A distribution made by a corporation to its shareholder generally of company earnings or surplus. Most dividends are taxable but exceptions are explained in (Lasser's) Chapter 3.

Earned income: Compensation for performing personal services. You must have earned income to make IRA contributions.

Estimated tax: Advance payment of current tax liability based either on wage withholdings or installment payments of your estimated tax liability. To avoid penalties, you generally must pay the IRS either 90% of your final tax liability, or 100% of the prior year's tax liability.

Fair market value: What a willing buyer would pay a willing seller when neither is under any compulsion to buy or sell.

Fiduciary: A person or corporation such as a trustee, executor or guardian who manages property for another person.

First-year expensing: A deduction of up to $10,000 of the cost of business equipment allowed in the year placed in service but subject to income and investment limits.

Fiscal year: A 12-month period ending on the last day of any month other than December. Partnerships, S corporations and personal service corporations are limited in their choice of fiscal years and face special restrictions.

401(k) Plan: A deferred pay plan, authorized by section 401(k) of the Internal Revenue Code under which a percentage of an employee's salary is withheld and placed in a savings account or the company's profit-sharing plan. The salary deferral is tax free if within an annual limitation, which is $7,313 for 1988. Income accumulates on the deferred amount until withdrawn by the employee at age 59 1/2 or when the employee retires or leaves the company.

Gross income: The total amount of income received from all sources before deductions.

Gross receipts: Total business receipts reported on Schedule C before deducting adjustments for returns and allowances and cost of goods sold.

Group-term life insurance: Employees are not taxed on up to $50,000 of group-term coverage financed by their employer.

Hobby loss: Expenses of a hobby are deductible only up to income from the activity; loss deductions are not allowed.

Independent contractor: A person who controls his or her own work and reports as a self-employed person.

Individual retirement account (IRA): A retirement account on which up to $2,000 may be contributed annually, but deductions for the contribution are restricted if you are covered by a company retirement plan. Earnings accumulate tax free on IRA contributions.

Innocent spouse: A spouse who claims that he or she should not be liable on joint return because of ignorance of the other spouse's omission of income or claiming of excessive writeoffs.

Keogh plan: Retirement plan set up by a self-employed person, providing tax deductible contributions, tax-free income accumulations until withdrawal and favorable averaging for qualifying lump-sum distributions.

Kiddie tax: The tax on the investment income of a dependent child under 14 in excess of $1,000, based on parents' marginal tax rate and computed on Form 8615.

Like-kind exchange: An exchange of similar assets used in a business or held for investment on which gain may be deferred.

Long-term capital gain or loss: Gain or loss on the sale or exchange of a capital asset held for more than six months if acquired before 1988, or for more than one year if acquired after 1987.

Luxury automobile limits: Ceiling placed on annual depreciation deductions for autos used for business.

Material participation tests: Rules for determining whether a person is active in a business activity for passive activity rule purposes. Unless the tests are met, passive loss limits apply.

Miscellaneous itemized deductions: Generally itemized deductions for job and investment expenses subject to a 2% adjusted gross income floor.

Mortgage interest: Fully deductible interest on up to two residences, if acquisition debt secured by home is $1 million or less, and home equity is $100,000 or less.

Net operating loss: Business loss which exceeds current income and which may be carried back against income of three prior years and carried forward as a deduction from future income for fifteen years until eliminated.

Ordinary and necessary: A legal requirement for deductibility of a business expense.

Ordinary income: Income other than capital gains.

Ordinary loss: A loss other than a capital loss.

Partnership: An unincorporated business or income producing entity organized by two or more persons. A partnership is not subject to tax but passes through to the partners all income, deductions, and credits, according to the terms of the partnership agreement.

Passive activity loss rules: Rules that limit the deduction of losses from passive activities to income from other passive activities. Passive activities include rental operations or businesses in which you do not materially participate.

Placed in service: The time when a depreciable asset is ready to be used. The date fixes the beginning of depreciation period.

Premature distributions: Withdrawals before age 59 1/2 from qualified retirement plans are subject to penalties unless specific exceptions are met.

Qualified plan: A retirement plan that meets tax law tests and allows for tax deferment and tax-free accumulation of income until benefits are withdrawn. Pension, profit-sharing, stock bonus, employee stock ownership, and Keogh plans and IRAs may be qualified plans.

Real property: Land and the buildings on the land. Buildings are depreciable.

Return of capital: A distribution of your investment that is not subject to tax unless the distribution exceeds your investment.

Rollover: A tax-free reinvestment of a distribution from a qualified retirement plan into an IRA or other qualified plan within 60 days after receipt.

Royalty income: Amounts received for the use of property such as mineral property, a book, a movie, or patent.

Salvage value: The estimated value of an asset at the end of its useful life.

S Corporation: A corporation that elects S status in order to receive tax treatment similar to a partnership.

Section 179 deduction: First-year expensing. A deduction of up to $10,000, allowed for investments in tangible depreciable property in the year the property is placed in service.

Self-employed person: An individual who operates a business or profession as a proprietor or independent contractor and reports self-employed income on Schedule C.

Self-employment tax: Tax paid by self-employed persons to finance social security coverage. In 1988, the rate is 13.02% on the first $45,000 of self-employment income.

Short-term capital gain or loss: Gain or loss on the sale or exchange of a capital asset held for six months or less, if property acquired before 1988, or held one year or less on property acquired after 1987.

Simplified employee plan (SEP): IRA-type plan set up by an employer, rather than the employee. Salary reduction contributions may be allowed to plans of small employers.

Standard mileage rate: A fixed rate allowed by the IRS for business auto expenses in place of deducting actual expenses.

Stock dividend: A corporate distribution of additional shares of its stock to its shareholders.

Straight-line method: A method of depreciating the cost of a depreciable asset on a pro-rata basis over its useful life.

Taxable income: Net income after claiming all deductions from gross income and adjusted gross income, such as IRA deductions, itemized deductions or the standard deduction and personal exemptions.

Tax deferral: Shifting income to a later year, such as where you defer taxable interest to the following year by purchasing a T-bill or savings certificate maturing after the end of the current year.

Tax home: The area of your principal place of business or employment. You must be away from your tax home on a business trip to deduct travel expenses.

Tax identification number: For an individual, his or her social security number; for businesses, fiduciaries, and other nonindividual taxpayers, employer identification number.

Tax year: A period of 12 months for reporting income and expenses.

Withholding: An amount taken from income as a pre-payment of an individual's tax liability for the year. In the case of wages, the employer withholds part of every wage payment. Backup withholding from dividend or interest income is required if you do not provide the payer with a correct taxpayer identification number. Withholding on pensions and IRA's is automatic unless you elect to waive withholding.

Bibliography

1988 Year-End Tax Planning: For Returns to be Filed in 1989. Chicago: Commerce Clearing House, Inc., 1984.

1989 Tax Guide for College Teachers. College Park, MD: Academic Information Service, Inc., 1988.

Ammer, Christine & Dean S. *Dictionary of Business and Economics.* New York: The Free Press, 1977, 461 pages.

Atkinson, William. *Working at Home: Is It for You?* Homewood, IL: Dow Jones-Irwin, 1985, 162 pages.

Block, Julian. "Putting a Family Member on the Payroll." *Home BusinessLine,* 2(10), 1, 8 (October, 1988).

Bock, C. Allen, et al. *1988 Farm Income Tax Schools Workbook.* Urbana, IL: The Illinois Cooperative Extension Service, November, 1988.

Brabec, Barbara. *Homemade Money: The Definitive Guide to Success in a Home Business.* White Hall, VA: Betterway Publications, Inc., 1986, 304 pages.

Brauner, David. "How to Start a Profitable Home Business," *Wealth Secrets,* pages 28–38 (February, 1989).

Browner, Emily and Henry Norr. "'Great fax modem hoax'?," *MacWeek,* 3(4), 19–20 (January 24, 1989).

Business Use of Your Home (Revised November 1988). Publication 587. Washington: Internal Revenue Service, 1988.

Calem, Rob. "What's New with Copiers?" *Home BusinessLine,* 2(10), 3 (October, 1988).

Christensen, Kathleen. "A Hard Day's Work in the Electronic Cottage." *Across The Board,* 24(4), 17–23 (April, 1987).

Collins, Eliza G. C. "A Company Without Offices." *Harvard Business Review*, 64(1), 127–136 (Jan/Feb 1986).

"Computers and the Work Place: Interest in Working at Home Still Strong." *Roper Reports*. New York: The Roper Organization, July, 1988, page 4.

Custer, Linda. "Laboratory Retrievers." *MacUser*, 4(7), 174–187 (July, 1988).

"Desktop Manufacturing." *Macworld*, 5(7), 81 (July, 1988).

"Desktop Video Takes Off." *Macworld*, 5(7), 81 (July, 1988).

"Developing a Sales Kit for Your Home-Based Business." *Home BusinessLine*, 2(9), 1, 3 (September, 1988).

Diamond, Michael R. and Julie L. Williams. *How to Incorporate: A Handbook For Entrepreneurs and Professionals*. New York: John Wiley & Sons, 1987, 242 pages.

Edwards, Paul and Sarah. *Working From Home*. Los Angeles: Tarcher, 1987, 436 pages.

Feldstein, Stuart. *Home, Inc*. New York: Grosset & Dunlap, 1981, 249 pages.

"First Color Separations." *Macworld*, 5(7), 75 (July, 1988).

Freff. "What It Isn't, What It Is." *MacUser*, 4(9), 265–266 (September, 1988).

Frohbieter-Mueller, Jo. *Stay Home and Mind Your Own Business*. White Hall, VA: Betterway Publications, Inc., 1987, 280 pages.

Froth, Edward C. and Ted D. Englebrecht. *S Corporations Guide*. Chicago: Commerce Clearing House, Inc., 1984.

"Getting the Most Out of the Property on Which You Work." *Home BusinessLine*, 2(9), 1, 8 (September, 1988).

"Getting the Most Out of Your Home Office Deductions." *Home BusinessLine*, 2(8), 1, 7 (August, 1988).

Goldstein, Arnold S. *Starting Your Subchapter "S" Corporation: How to Build a Business the Right Way*. New York: John Wiley & Sons, 1988, 182 pages.

Hawken, Paul. *Growing A Business*. New York: Simon & Schuster, 1987, 251 pages.

Hedberg, Augustin. "Writing Off a Home Office: Is it a Brilliant Deduction or an Annual Nightmare?" *Money*, 18(2), 41–44 (February 1989).

Hilson, William E. "Desktop Publishing: the High-tech Tool for Home-Based Businesses." *Home BusinessLine*, 2(9), 2, 7 (September 1988).

Hoeber, Ralph C., et al. *Contemporary Business Law Principles and Cases*. New York: McGraw-Hill, 1980, 1139 pages.

Home Offices & Workspaces, the Editors of Sunset Books and Sunset Magazine. Menlo Park, CA: Sunset-Lane Publishing Company, 1986. 96 pages.

Horvath, Francis W. "Work at home: new findings from the Current Population Survey." *Monthly Labor Review*, 109(11), 31–35 (November, 1986).

J. K. Lasser's Your Income Tax 1989. New York: Simon & Schuster, 1988, 501 pages.

Jordan, Joanna. *How to Get Rich Sooner Than You Think, Volumes 1 & 2.* Sterling, VA: New Start Publications, Inc., 1987, 108/122 pages.

Kelly, Marcia M. "Telecommuting: The Next Workplace Revolution." *Information Strategy,* 2(2), 20–23 (Winter 1986)

Kelly, Robert E. *The Gold Collar Worker.* Reading, MA: Addison-Wesley, 1985, 196 pages.

Kotite, Erika. "Homebased Hints." *Entrepreneur,* 17(3), 126–134 (March, 1989).

Kotite, Erika. "The 30-Second Commute." *Entrepreneur,* 17(3), 118–124 (March, 1989).

Lehrman, Paul D. "Scroll Over Beethoven." *MacUser,* 4(7), 210–224 (July, 1988).

Lesberg, Eileen. *Observations,* An Information Service of World Wide Facilities, Inc., Garden City, NY, Premiere Issue, Number One, undated (circa 1987), 4 pages.

Levine, Joanne. "Home Office Equipment." *Incentive,* 162(5), 124–128 (May, 1988).

Moffatt, Terry. "The Facts About The Fax." *Vis a Vis,* 3(2), 45–54 (February, 1989).

O'Conner, Anne Marie. "Fax Machines for the Home-Based Business User." *Home BusinessLine,* 2(8), 1, 6, 8 (August, 1988).

O'Conner, Anne Marie. "Keogh Plans: The Retirement Programs Designed for the Self-Employed." *Home BusinessLine,* 2(10), 1, 7–8 (October, 1988).

Operating Home-Based Businesses in Military Housing. Washington: Department of Defense, 1988, pamphlet.

Pace, Ben F. and Ann T. *The Complete Direct Mail Business Manual.* Baton Rouge, LA: Solomon Reid, Ltd., 1987, 133 pages.

Peltz, David L. "2-D CAD: A Landscape View." *Macworld,* 5(7), 118–126 (July, 1988).

Pollan, Stephen M. & Mark Levine. "Playing to Win: The Small Business Guide to Survival and Growth." Special Advertising Section prepared in cooperation with U. S. Chamber of Commerce, *U.S. News & World Report,* 1988, 32 pages.

"Prentice Hall's Explanation of the Technical and Miscellaneous Revenue Act of 1988." *Federal Tax Guide.* Paramus, NJ: Prentice Hall, November 7, 1988.

Research Institute Master Federal Tax Manual: 1989 Edition. Blacksburg, VA: Cooperative Extension Service, VPI & SU, 1988.

Risk Management and Business Insurance. New York: Insurance Information Institute, 1988, 13 pages.

Risk Management: A Small Business Primer. Washington: U. S. Chamber of Commerce, 1987, 78 pages.

Robinson, Phillip. "Desktop Engineering." *MacUser,* 4(7), 136–153 (July, 1988).

Savage, J. A. "California Smog Fuels Telecommuting Plans." *Computerworld*, 22(18), 65–66 (May 2, 1988).

Schill, Charlie. "Pentagon Now Encourages Home-Based Businesses." *Navy Times*. Springfield, VA: Army Times Publishing Co., 38th Year, No. 8, December 5, 1988, page 10.

Scott, Robert. "Playing by the Rules: Regulations Affecting the Home-Based Business." *Home BusinessLine*, 2(9), 1, 4–6 (September, 1988).

Shapiro, Ezra. "Publish or Perish." *MacUser*, 4(8), 149–152 (August, 1988).

Small Business: Building America's Future. Washington: U. S. Chamber of Commerce, 1988, 35 pages.

Storey, M. John. *Starting Your Own Business: No Money Down*. New York: Wiley, 1987, 266 pages.

Tax Guide for Small Business (Revised November 1988). Publication 334. Washington: Internal Revenue Service, 1988.

Tax Withholding and Estimated Tax (Revised December 1988). Publication 505. Washington: Internal Revenue Service, 1988.

Telecommunications Ideas to Grow On: A Planning Tool for Small Business Growth. Basking Ridge, NJ: AT&T, 1986, 8 pages.

Telecommunications Ideas to Grow On: Capitalizing on Money Management. Basking Ridge, NJ: AT&T, 1986, 8 pages.

Telecommunications Ideas to Grow On: Expanding Your Markets. Basking Ridge, NJ: AT&T, 1986, 11 pages.

Telecommunications Ideas to Grow On: Improving Your Field Sales Productivity. Basking Ridge, NJ: AT&T, 1986, 12 pages.

Telecommunications Ideas to Grow On: Keeping Customers Satisfied. Basking Ridge, NJ: AT&T, 1986, 11 pages.

"The Agent, His Independent Contractor Status and the IRS." *MANA Research Bulletin*, No. 542, Laguna Hills, CA: Manufacturers' Agents National Association, 1983, 4 pages.

The Light Book: A Guide for Lighting Your Home. Cleveland, OH: General Electric, 1988, 36 pages.

The Small Business Resource Guide. Washington: Braddock Communications, Inc., 1988, 135 pages. (an SBA & AT&T initiative)

Tomczak, Steven P. *Successful Consulting for Engineers and Data Processing Professionals*. New York: John Wiley & Sons, 1982, 335 pages.

Tooley, Jo Ann. "Leaving the Office Nest." *U.S. News & World Report*, 105(25), 120 (December 26, 1988/January 2, 1989).

Waymon, Lynne. *Starting and Managing a Business from Your Home*. Washington: U. S. Small Business Administration, 1986, 48 pages.

Weaver, Peter. *You, Inc.* Garden City, NY: Dolphin Books, 1975, 299 pages.

Westin, Richard A. *Lexicon of Tax Terminology*. New York: John Wiley & Sons, 1984.

Wolfson, Richard. "Milling Around." *MacUser,* 4(7), 188–196 (July, 1988).

Working at Home, the Editors of Better Homes and Gardens. Des Moines, IA: Meredith Corporation, 1985, 160 pages.

Yavelow, Christopher. "Music Processing: The Next Generation." *Macworld,* 5(7), 102–111 (July, 1988).

Your Federal Income Tax (Revised November 1988). Publication 17. Washington: Internal Revenue Service, 1988.

Your Guide to USAA Services, 1989 Edition. San Antonio: USAA, 1988.

Index